D1242803

The Civilization of Christianity

The Civilization of Christianity

JOHN L. McKENZIE

THE THOMAS MORE PRESS
Chicago, Illinois

ACKNOWLEDGMENT:
Excerpt from ON BEING A CHRISTIAN by Hans Kung.
Copyright © 1976 by Doubleday & Company, Inc. Reprinted by permission of the publisher.

Hardcover ISBN 0-88347-180-9

Contents

To the memory of
PHYLLIS ANNE JOHNSON
(1937-1885)

And to
ROSEMARY KATHLEEN WEISBROD ROBINSON
For her thirteenth birthday

ACKNOWLEDGMENTS

I extend my thanks to the Rev. Michael Duffy, M. M., to the Rev. Lee Klosinski, C.S.C., and to Josephine Merrill Kirkpatrick, for a careful and critical reading of the MS. Many of their suggestions are incorporated into the work; they will recognize them more in what has been omitted than in what is written. They did the kind of work which we used to hope for from censors. My thanks are gratefully tendered to the editorial staff of the Thomas More Association, who accepted both the idea of the work and the completed MS., and saw to its editing and publishing. Many of their suggestions also have been incorporated into the work. I am more grateful to Anita Weisbrod Robinson and to her daughter Rosemary for their tolerance of an aging and sometimes grumpy author. It is a small return to offer the book to Rosemary as a gift for her thirteenth birthday. Though I doubt that she will read the work at once, when she does, I expect some searching questions about what I have written.

My neighbor and colleague and good friend, Dr. Phyllis A. Johnson, was taken by an untimely death on April 9, 1985. Her loss is felt keenly by all her friends and associates; I feel especially deprived because I had counted on the painfully honest and critical reading which she would have given the MS. of this book. To her memory I dedicate this book.

John L. McKenzie
June 8, 1985
Claremont, California

PREFACE AND APOLOGY

THERE are many good reasons why an author should not begin another book in his seventy-fourth year. Apart from the bare fact of physical and mental fatigue, there is the great probability (to which his friends may mistakenly be too kind to attest) that one, like a field or a mine, is worked out; he may have said all that he has to say. There is also the great probability (for me it is a certainty) that because of age and weariness one has let the always moving procession of scholarship move ahead of one. There are other reasons; but the reason which carries the greatest weight for me is the extremely bad track record of authors who have clung too long to the pen (or the typewriter or the word processor). I remember reading years ago about the justly renowned and admired Adolf von Harnack, who was still writing in his eighties. What he was then producing was not the kind of work which had made Harnack a household word (at least in the households of theologians) thirty years earlier. It was writing so closely supervised and corrected by his graduate assistants that they were the real authors; and competent as they may have been, they were not Harnack. Neither was he; the man who had shaken theology to its roots was no longer alive. I remember reading one of those products of his golden years. The first page had one line of text; the rest of the page was footnotes. Footnotes, my colleagues may tell me, have never been enough of a problem for me; I shall not discourage my readers with that kind of senile rambling. Other kinds I cannot promise to spare them.

With all these and other excellent reasons for not doing what I am starting to do, why do I not enjoy a leisurely and quiet retirement like so many of my peers? Let me suggest that there are some books which one is unable to write until one has counted three score and ten years. This book, as much as any I ever wrote (and more than most), arises from an inner compulsion. It arises from what Juvenal called with more wit than elegance the *cacoethes scribendi,* the itch to write. I think it was in the same context that the same Roman versifier wrote *Facit indignatio versus,* which I may render: I am so angry that I have to write. It will be my task to set forth why I am so wrought up and to justify my belief that the causes of my intellectual and emotional disturbance deserve publication in a book. Once I recognized the condition for what it was, all I needed was a publisher who was willing to take the risk involved. I am responsible for writing the book; Dan Herr, Joel Wells and Todd Brennan of the Thomas More Association are responsible for the transmission of the manuscript to the printed page. For the purpose of getting the manuscript into a book they are the most important of the friends beyond number to whom I have set forth as a topic for discussion the central thesis of the book. I have also proposed the thesis before some lecture audiences. I have tried to incorporate their responses in my treatment of the topic. One will recognize it as a topic which is both extremely broad and profoundly implicated in many contemporary issues (probably including some of which I am unaware) and has not to my knowledge been treated formally and explicitly by anyone else. I cannot pretend to have read everything, and for that I do not believe an apology is necessary.

I think the origins of the book lie somewhere around 1948. In 1943 I began to teach the interpretation of the Old Testament in a seminary (after less than proper time of preparation in graduate studies; if you have forgotten, there was a war going on). Among the prophets I chose for exposition were the books of Isaiah and Jeremiah; Amos was also relevant to the problem burgeoning in my mind. In 1948 the Second World War was only three years in the past; unless one is old enough to remember it, one cannot realize the warm glow of self-righteousness in which the western world was bathed. We, the good guys, had successfully beaten into a pulp the bad guys. Anyone who says that his theological thinking rises serenely above the turmoil of contemporary events is lying in his teeth. There were a very few who raised their voices in question about the purity of us Galahads—who asked about the use of the nuclear bomb, about some of our ethics in waging war and in imposing peace. Like all my contemporaries on the seminary faculties, I had been reared on the ethics of the just war. It was about this time that I devised for my students a parallel between the just war and the just adultery, to which I shall return later. This analogy never worked well with audiences because they, like me, had been trained in the traditional Catholic morality: while killing a man or a woman is morally neutral, bedding one of the opposite sex is *intrinsece et per se* evil.

But I leap ahead of my story slightly. It was in 1948 that President Truman (to whom we owe the first and second and so far the last use of the nuclear bomb) was reelected, and almost at once the Cold War in which we are still engaged was begun. Such things did not enter into the exposition of the theology of the prophets any more than the incessant hammering outside the classroom did; I suspect that most of the surviving students remember the hammering better than anything I said. It was just impossible to dull one's awareness either of the Cold War or of the hammering. It seemed very likely that in a short time we would be involved in a war (the third to end all wars since I was born) and we were girding our moral loins for another struggle between the good guys (us) and the bad guys (them). And I found that I could not expound Isaiah and Jeremiah without running headlong into some things which were very dear and very sacred in the world in which I lived.

For if there is one thing which emerges with total clarity from First Isaiah and Jeremiah (who has not yet been pro-toed and deuteroed, if you will pardon the expression), it is the unqualified conviction that the ancient kingdom of Judah would sin by defending itself against Assyria and Babylon. It is also quite clear that this had nothing to do with the moral rectitude of Assyria and Babylon, whom the prophets recognized as predatory and oppressive ex-ploiters of their victims. It is also clear that it had every-thing to do with the moral inadequacy of Judah, which had not even the most flimsy justification for defending itself. From my efforts to present what I believed the books contained arose my convinced pacifism, which has endured to this day. It has flourished in spite of intelligent and determined opposition from the time when I first essayed its presentation. I have convinced a few listeners, or, to tell the truth, they convinced themselves.

I have become aware of the obvious evasions which most of us employ when we are confronted with such a clear biblical statement. The rest of the book will be largely devoted to what is ambitiously intended to be a devastating criticism of these and similar evasions. It will probably fail because we are comfortable with these evasions. But at the moment, since I am telling how the idea of this book came into my mind, I must dwell briefly on something which I shall expand in later pages. The most common evasion, as well as the easiest, is that the prophets did not speak to us or to our situation, and that we must devise a new morality by which we can solve an entirely new set of problems. This evasion takes many forms; it is serpentine, it is a hydra, and it comes down to a declaration that we have created a new species to whom the past can say nothing. I wonder whether Isaiah and Jeremiah did not hear some version of this from their contemporaries. For that matter, I wonder if Adam and Eve did not hear something like this from Cain explaining what had happened to Abel. It seems that we cannot learn from the experience of the past because what has happened to us has never happened to anyone before.

Let me return to a sentence which appeared a few lines above. I said that we were all taught the traditional Catholic morality that while killing a person is morally neutral, bedding him or her is intrinsically evil. I meant that we may find moral reasons for doing away with a person (for instance, he or she may approach me with a weapon and the manifest intention to use it). But we can never find a moral justification for bedding the person except marriage. When I proposed my analogy half-seriously nearly forty years ago, I never thought that I would live long enough to see carnal intercourse become both in scholarly and in popular opinion as morally neutral as killing. Modern science and philosophy have made of carnal intercourse a "meaningful interpersonal relation," and this is the discovery which makes the past irrelevant for the new species we have created. To me the meaningful interpersonal relation is just as phony a piece of morality as the just war. I call them both phony because both show an essential disrespect for the dignity of the human person, which I am old-fashioned enough to believe is made in God's image, and thus differs from dogs and cats. To anticipate what I shall try to set forth with what length and depth the topic deserves, this disrespect is what I believe to be the essentially unchristian feature of all moralities past and present.

Perhaps this disquisition will give some idea of the *malaise* which I have felt through most of the forty years of teaching biblical interpretation and biblical theology, of publishing more books and articles on these topics than I care to remember, of numerous excursions to lecture platforms on several continents, and of appearances in widely scattered pulpits in which I posed as a preacher of the word of God. The *malaise* was hard to specify, but it was there—like a pebble in the shoe, like a dripping faucet, like a squeak in the car. Unlike these, it could not easily be spotted. It took me the better part of fifty years to recognize that my *malaise* was a deliberately unrecognized discord between what I was and the word of God which I had so long studied (even the self-taught learn something), taught and written about not entirely without success or distinction or, to be candid, profit. My way of life and my world demanded the maintenance of a number of assumptions which the word of God compelled me to question. My way of life and my world did not permit me to ask those questions. When the questions grew to an intolerable number, this book was the only way to find comfort, the comfort which I hope is reached by at last achieving total candor. If this gets done, I will no longer have anything to hide.

So why should this moral purgation be inflicted on an unsuspecting world? I will not say an innocent world. It is a world and a way of life which I have shared with thousands: Jesuits (thirty-eight years of my adult life),

Catholic priests (forty-five years at this writing), professors and scholars on the level of higher education (forty-three years) and authors (my first book appeared in 1956). Anything unusual or scandalous must have occurred before 1928, and there is almost no one left to deny my declaration that there was nothing of the sort. I am obliged to write this for my colleagues, who, in my knowledge and experience, have not realized, as I finally did, that they are wolves in sheep's clothing or whited sepulchres, to borrow a couple of phrases from one whom we profess to regard as one of our heroes. I shall have a few things to say about this alleged hero-worship. It is our refusal to recognize the discord of which I speak that is possibly most responsible for the sustained disharmony of what the Greeks called the *ecumene,* the world in which men and women live.

I have spoken of the word of God, which I do not limit to the canonical Scriptures. My brief publications on this topic have not satisfied all my readers that I really believe in the divine inspiration of the Scriptures. It would not satisfy them to reaffirm my belief that God was involved in the composition of these books as he was not involved in the composition of other books (such as this one, or the *Iliad),* and it would be too much for others who believe that God was as much involved in the composition of the Scriptures as he was in the composition of other books (such as this one, or the *Iliad*). So, since I am not writing to please anyone except myself, I shall let my belief in the inspiration of the Scriptures stand as I have just stated it with no further argument. It is because of this belief, and not because of any alleged literary or theological merits of the Scriptures, that I have been able to live with the study of the Scriptures for nearly fifty years. Let me say at once that if literary and theological merit had been what I sought, I could have lived just as happily for nearly fifty years with the corpus of Byzantine literature. One finds some rare pieces; but they are, as Jerome said about the apocryphal books, like finding pearls in the mud. For one Psalm 23 there are dozens like Psalm 119. At moments when reading the Bible seems like Elijah's forty days walk to Mount Horeb, I have wondered whether any purpose would be served by a catalogue of books and passages which have escaped deserved oblivion only because they were venerated as sacred. To preserve faith in the divine inspiration of the Scriptures is easy if one never reads them. For the professional exegete it is a task. I wonder whether God is flattered by having such monumental bad taste and literary incompetence attributed to him as are exhibited in much of the sacred Scriptures.

I have been asked more than once whether I still believe what I profess as a Catholic, or whether I am a practicing Catholic, or why I do not resign from the Catholic priesthood and the Catholic Church and go where I belong, wherever that may be. This question is so rude that I have found a rude answer to be the best answer; since my readers, far from being rude, have been kind enough to bear with me up to this point, I respond with two well worn anecdotes. You could call them parables. The first concerns an Irish writer (James Joyce, I think). When asked whether he had abandoned Catholicism for Protestantism, he answered (forgive the attempt to reproduce the brogue), "Sure and it's me faith I renounced, not me reason." The second concerns two professional gamblers who conducted their business aboard Mississippi River steamboats. When a steamer carrying them had to put in for repairs at a small remote village for a number of hours, they went ashore with the other passengers and became separated. When they rejoined each other some hours later, one found the other engaged in a local card game. The observer watched the play for a few minutes, and at the first opportunity he whispered to the player, "Listen, Jim, this game is crooked." Jim whispered back, "I know it's crooked, but it's the only game in town." That answer might not satisfy John Paul II or the Roman Curia, but it satisfies me, and I have to live with myself, not with them.

This leads to another, which is perhaps the only important question: what do you think of Jesus? I believe I owe it to myself and to my readers to answer with frankness as complete as I can make it, and without evasion. I believe Jesus is the most important and the most significant human being who ever lived. I believe that he is now truly alive as no one who ever lived and died is truly alive. I believe, to borrow a phrase which I once read in the writings of Rudolf Bultmann (and I can no longer find it), that Jesus realized the possibilities of human existence more than any other human being. I believe that all I think I know about God is derived from what Jesus was, said and did. I believe that the little we have left of what he said and did tells us more about how we can now in our world realize the possibilities of human existence than all the wisdom of the past and present—that is, he tells us something about how to live which no one else has ever told us. I apply to him what the late Vince Lombardi said about winning: Jesus is not an important person, he is the only person. I suspect I am what some of my younger colleagues would call a Christomonist. If anyone thinks these superlatives are exaggerated, let him suggest some other as a replacement to whom they rightly or equally belong. The rest of this book will attempt to furnish some basis for Christomonism, if one must call it that.

A few other questions may come up; I shall discuss them now briefly, reserving fuller discussion for the time if and when it becomes necessary. I am convinced that Jesus rejected the title Christ or Messiah (from which we get the denomination Christian). This is unfortunate. The ineradicable existence of this appellation serves to remind us that from the beginning his followers tried to make him something he was not, as we still do. Do I believe that he was and is God, or the Son of God? The New Testament never calls him the first. As to the second, I believe his personal relation with the deity (his Father) could be communicated to no one else. Whether this imposes the Chalcedonian Christology upon me is not clear to me; this Christology was devised for believers who had problems which I do not have, and it implies a number of philosophical presuppositions which I do not share. I recite the creed liturgically without reservations as a profession of our common Catholic faith which I share with no understanding that it says all that can be known about Jesus. I do not think anyone ever said that it does. In my experience the theological danger threatening modern Catholics (and indeed most post-Chalcedonian Catholics) is not a doubt that Jesus was and is God, but a doubt that Jesus was and is man; this means a doubt that anything he was, did or said is meaningful to the human race in the human condition.

These are my presuppositions, stated with enough fullness to undertake the discourse; as the thesis of the book unfolds, it will be necessary to restate some of them more fully and to deal with some objections. My purpose at the beginning is to leave as little doubt as possible in the reader's mind about where I stand in my religious faith and in my theological positions. I must now state as clearly as brevity will permit the thesis which this book is going to set forth and defend. Those who think that the thesis is impossible to defend or even to state may stop reading after this paragraph; they may join those who will not grant my presuppositions even for the sake of argument (in logic this is called transmission). The thesis is that there is a deadly and irreconcilable opposition between western civilization and Christianity and that one of them must destroy the other. My presuppositions do not allow me to believe that Christianity will not survive this conflict. The first step in the exposition will be to state clearly and definitely what I mean by western civilization and what I mean by Christianity. If I cannot identify these two historic realities, there can be no talk of a conflict. I am aware that my definitions may beg the question; but I think that any effort to define these two terms may beg the question by defining them according to the values which the disputant brings to the discussion. I fear that for members of the two historic communities of which I speak an objective and impartial definition (shall we say purely scientific?) of these terms has long been impossible. Nor do I think membership in another community such as the Jewish, the Moslem, the Indian or the Chinese would liberate the disputant from preconceived values and prejudices. It would almost certainly equip the disputant with a new and different set of presuppositions. I intend to speak of things which I said earlier are very dear and very sacred to members of the world in which I live. Perhaps one cannot know that one has made a valid point unless one treads upon toes and hears an indignant yell of pain.

This thesis, as I said above, has long been growing—or shall I say festering?—in my mind. In teaching, writing, lecturing and preaching I found myself more and more frequently abstaining from topics and developments which were legitimate or even necessary derivations from the word of God because I thought that readers or listeners were not ready for them. What I really meant was that I was not ready to say them. To say these things would demand revisions in conventional thought and behavior which neither I nor most of the people I know either by personal acquaintance or by reading their writings were willing to make. "Accepted conventional thought and behavior" is a very large basket; it will be my purpose to specify and to particularize some of these conventional patterns. I have no doubt that accepted conventional patterns of thought and behavior more often than not keep one from making a damn fool of oneself; is there not at times a worry that they may ensure that one is making a damn fool of oneself, or something worse—making a villain of oneself? Is this what Plato meant when he said that the unexamined life is not worth living? Our younger contemporaries are fond of blaming society rather than the individual for anything that they think is wrong; my treatment should please them, because I have picked as a target the biggest social reality of all—until they find that I do not spare individuals. I will add, paraphrasing Edmund Burke, that society is the last refuge of scoundrels. Over the course of the years I became assured that the first reason I am not an authentic Christian is that I do not choose to be one. The second reason, which I always felt it was in my power to overcome, was my culture—my fellow men and women—which makes it nearly impossible to be an authentic Christian and very easy to be one of several attractive alternatives. My position is simply the position of the child in Hans Christian Andersen's story: the emperor has no clothes on. I recognize that my colleagues and I are the emperor's tailors. The conventions of which I speak have compelled me (and I was a willing victim) to be cowardly and dishonest for most of my life. Let my colleagues appease their consciences, if they have one, in their own way; I am old enough, God knows, to say what I think and not what I am told or permitted to say. In past years I have had some disagreeable encounters with ecclesiastical censors. For these encounters I won a few tributes for courage; but thank you, no—I do not really deserve them. When I met the unofficial censors of conventional scholarship, I folded like a camp stool. When I was told to jump, my only question was "How high?"

This conventional and accepted pattern of thought and methodology is what is called the mainstream of scholarship. This is also the unofficial censorship of my scholarly colleagues which I have sometimes felt and silently rebelled against. Now that I am burning what I have so long adored, I find I do it with mixed feelings. Like Edna St. Vincent Millay's candle, the flame will not last the night, but it gives a lovely light. Nearly forty years ago one of my colleagues in the seminary said I was attacking Thomism with the weapons it has given me. I thought I was making progress in new directions with those weapons in dealing with problems which traditional Thomism had not encountered. I know now that to say there are new problems is to attack your traditions; and I am doing it again. I never had any intellectual tools except the tools of classical Thomism; to attempt to destroy it would be to attempt self-destruction. Similarly, the mainstream of conventional scholarship is what has so long enabled me to stay afloat and even to attempt some timid swimming, self-propelled and self-directed. Without this support I cannot move, I cannot even open my mouth or breathe. Let my readers remember this if they read on. Those who have shared my life in the mainstream know that the current is swift and strong, that it sets the direction of travel and the limits of adventure, that it is unforgiving to those who attempt to swim against its flow. Well, hell, let's go; I have nothing to lose but my chains.

The reader will find that the normal thread of discourse is occasionally interrupted by the appearance of other literary forms, mostly snatches of dialogue. The reader may wonder why I no longer find straight expository prose a vehicle good enough for my purposes, or whether this is not a sign of the feebleness associated with age which I mentioned earlier. Let me say that the dialogue as a vehicle of exposition is sufficiently long established; the Egyptian Dialogue of a Man with his Soul appeared shortly after 2000 B.C., fifteen hundred years before Plato. The whole book could have been written in dialogue form, since the essence of the book is confrontation. I choose to stick with what I have done so often, knowing that I am not Plato and that his clothes might not fit me, while I satisfy a life-long desire to play with my topic; just say it is a septuagenarian kid. The characters of the dialogue I have derived from that mysterious source known to my colleagues as Q. And since I am absolutely safe in saying that Q in the passages which I echo wrote fiction, who would quarrel with me for following in the steps of such a venerable predecessor? Q gives me the characters Satan, who I have chosen to call Nick ("Old Nick" to his friends), and Yeshu; I shrink from putting words in the mouth of Jesus. I have taken the liberty to expand the temptations and alter the scenes somewhat. The student of the Bible will recognize that I have written haggadic midrash, a type of edifying fiction (at least in intention). I do not believe in the reality of a personal superhuman Evil Spirit; I do believe in the reality which Satan symbolizes, and I believe that reality has a human face. Nick and Yeshu are both dramatic fictions. Nick is the human figure who represents the genius of western civilization. Whom does Yeshu represent? If I really knew that, I would have written a different and a much better book. Comparing the book with the topic, I echo the despairing verdict on his own work which legend attributes to Thomas Aquinas, delivered on his deathbed:

VIDETUR MIHI SICUT PALEA

I paraphrase, I think with utter fidelity to what he meant: It looks to me like a pile of the stuff usually found on the floors of stables.

TEMPTATION I: IN THE DESERT

IT is late afternoon in the Jordan valley near the shores of the Dead Sea. At this hour the sun has already fallen below the mountains of Judea, which tower sharply to the west to an altitude of 3500 feet above where we are, and the intolerably humid heat which blankets this region most of the year has begun to lessen. As is normal in this desolate area, there appears to be no human being in sight. A solitary figure emerges. He looks like a Jew, which would not make him unusual here. He is dressed in a single garment, the tunic or gown worn by all, male and female. He wears the beard and long hair characteristic of all Palestinian Jews. His skin is burnt by the sun: his tunic and his person show the dust which has accumulated over several days of exposure in the desert. He is gaunt and appears to be fatigued. He seats himself on a rock and gazes across the valley to where the mountains east of the river still shine in the rays of the declining sun.

He sees that he is not alone. Another figure appears; as he draws near, he is seen to be another young man, like the first, in the fullness of his maturity. In other respects he is completely dissimilar. He is wearing the toga of a Roman gentleman; he is clean shaven and wears his hair closely cropped in the style of a Roman gentleman. He is handsome and strong; far from gaunt, he seems to be in perfect physical condition. Like his toga, he is spotlessly clean; in spite of the oppressive heat he looks as if he has just stepped from a refreshing bath. His appearance in this bleak desert is as paradoxical as would be the appearance of the young Jew in the palace of the Caesars. As he stands before the young man, they survey each other with cool and fearless calm. The Roman speaks:

24

STRANGER: A good afternoon to you, Yeshu son of Joseph.

YESHU: And a good afternoon to you, sir.

STRANGER: What are you doing in this God-forsaken place?

YESHU: I might ask you the same question. It may be a strange thing I am doing, but I came here to find out who I am.

STRANGER: It is a strange thing, and most people would do well to spend more time doing it. John the Baptizer bothered you, didn't he?

YESHU: It goes back farther than that; but since you know so much about me, I feel you have the advantage of me until you tell me who you are.

STRANGER: That I will do; but first of all, let me tell you that I came here looking for you. I think I can help you; if I cannot tell you who you are, I can tell you who you can become.

YESHU: And you can tell me how you got here looking so clean and fresh. It bothers me; I wonder whether you might have come something like Elijah in reverse, but I did not see any chariot.

STRANGER: We have a few techniques we are not quite ready to go public with. I am able to offer you right now what you want most, a big drink of cold water, followed by an equally big drink of chilled wine from Chios (none of your Palestinian rotgut) and a refreshing supper according to your order. I know you have been fasting for a few weeks. This will show you that I mean what I say and can deliver on what I promise.

YESHU: No, thanks.

STRANGER: No? maybe you would like to turn these rocks into your supper. You're hungry, and it is an offer made in kindness; don't be churlish.

YESHU: I am sorry if I appear churlish. But your offer of a Roman supper in this God-forsaken place, as you call it, has something funny about it. It sounds like the work of Adonai himself or You-Know-Who, and you have not proved that this supper comes from Adonai. Maybe it's the Jewishness in me, but I don't think Adonai would send one of his angels dressed like a Roman gentleman. And you have not yet told me who you are.

STRANGER: All right. I have been around quite a long

time, and I have several titles in different places where I have property. But skip those; my name is Nicholas. My friends call me Nick—Old Nick.

YESHU: Well, sir Nicholas—

NICK: Nick, please; we have to do business on a friendly basis.

YESHU: Well, Nick; suppose you tell me why you came looking for me, and how you can help me find out what I can become.

NICK: I said I have property in a lot of places. I am always looking for good men to take jobs as managers of my interests. Let me say that while I am not as well known as some Roman magnates—I like to keep it that way—there is no man in the world who has the resources I have, or who can reward his managers as I can and do. Name what you want, and it's yours.

YESHU: You make it sound as if Adonai himself could not pay better.

NICK: Adonai is not famous for paying his employees well. You will find this hard to believe, but Adonai and I made an arrangement a long time ago. You can read about it in the Torah. Adonai told me, "The world belongs to you. Take charge of it.''

YESHU: I know the place. I thought he said that to
              Adam.

NICK: That is one of my titles. In Greek they call
              me Anthropos. That is my business, carry-
              ing out that saying of Adonai. My busi-
              ness is to subdue the earth. I represent
              Mankind, with a capital letter. The work
              is slow, and sometimes I think the biggest
              obstacle I have is people. That is why I am
              always looking for men and women of
              great natural gifts like you. If you work
              for me, there is no degree of power which
              you cannot have if you show that you can
              carry the responsibility. I could tell you
              stories of men who could not carry the
              load they assumed; they wanted the
              rewards without doing the work.

YESHU: You seem to have a lot of subduing still
              to do.

NICK: Yeshu, I have plans for mankind so big
              you could not understand them, smart as I
              think you are. The Romans think they
              have the world licked; I can't tell them
              they don't even know how big it is. And
              there is no way I can tell them that com-
              pared to what I have in mind they are
              really primitive. It takes time, it takes

work, and it takes good people; that is why I am here. I want you.

YESHU: You do not want a simple village carpenter from Nazareth. Who ever came from Nazareth that amounted to anything? If you want a smart Jew, you will find plenty of them in Alexandria, or even a few in Jerusalem.

NICK: Do not worry; I can give you anything you need except talent, and you have that from Adonai. Think of it, Yeshu; it is the biggest thing a man can get into, he can do more for more people, and it will last longer than anything else you could do. Yeshu, a man like you ought to think big; I can make it possible for you to *do* big. You owe it to your fellow human beings to realize the possibilities which Adonai has given you to enrich the world, to make it a better place to live. You will commit a sin by letting God-given talent rot in this rat-hole of Palestine.

YESHU: And I suppose it will also give me a chance to enrich myself and make the world a better place for me to live in?

NICK: I make no foolish promises; I make opportunities, and it is for you to realize them. People who work for me have to work very hard, and many of them find that success is pleasure enough. They work hard at creating and diffusing good things and beautiful things. They are in a position to control the good and the beautiful, and it is up to them how good and beautiful they want to make their lives. I do not interfere.

YESHU: The late king Herod—did he work for you?

NICK: Not one of my outstanding employees—but yes, he did. And before you go on to say what you are thinking, please bear in mind that he cleaned up a very rotten situation. You are not old enough to remember the Hasmoneans and the way they wrecked the country. And he built some of the finest buildings since Solomon, another of my employees. No, Herod did what had to be done when it had to be done. He saved this country and its people; I suppose you, a Jew, think they were worth saving. But I expect far more from you than I got from Herod; he had a bit of a heavy hand—no finesse, shall we say? Augustus (there, Yeshu, was a man of whom I am proud) said that it was better to be Herod's sow than his son.

YESHU: Did Herod's son and grandson work for you too?

NICK: Please do not mention those swine; I got rid of them. I demand a certain level of competence in my employees. But complete self-dedication like those—I cannot use them, Yeshu.

YESHU: Suppose I did not want to do the kind of work for you which Herod and Augustus did—and I suppose Tiberius, the present Caesar, works for you too?

NICK: He either works for me or he is not Caesar. But Yeshu, there is almost no human activity in which I cannot use people who do their work well. I can use artists, philosophers like the late Cicero in Rome (no Plato, but he should have stuck to philosophy and stayed out of politics), poets like those in the employ of Augustus, Horace and Virgil. I think you could write something as good as they did if you put your mind to it. I do not fuss with the trivia, the jobs which anyone can do; there I do not have to look for any special people. I need people of great talent in the important positions in the world to get the job well done. Remember it is the welfare of the human race, the advancement of man's rule over the world which all these people are engaged in. I think I can say that Adonai has committed to me the charge of every important and valuable activity that man—my namesake-

—carries on. I can find something you like and can do and give you everything you need to get it done.

YESHU: Nick, I am not as smart as you are; I am just a country boy. But in Nazareth we think that no one, even a man wearing a fancy Roman toga, ever comes along and offers us something for nothing. What is your game?

NICK: All right, I will lay it on the line. What I want from you is complete and undivided loyalty, the same thing I want from everyone who works for me.

YESHU: Complete and undivided? You will have to specify, Nick.

NICK: You are smart, Yeshu, and I think you already grasp the scope of my enterprises. It is the advancement of man to complete supremacy over the world. Everything you do must work for that, and you must do or allow nothing to happen which blocks or impedes it. You may make mistakes as long as they are mistakes made in the right direction—let us call them excesses of zeal in pushing the cause—and I will help you repair them; but mistakes of slackness, of softness—I do not tolerate them and I do not forgive. Is that clear?

YESHU: Clearer than you think, Nick.

NICK: Then why don't we step aboard the craft I have just behind that hillock (the chariot you did not see, Yeshu) and close the agreement over supper?

YESHU: No.

NICK: What?

YESHU: Get lost, Nick.

NICK: Yeshu, no one turns me down and gets away with it. Did anyone ever tell you about an Athenian named Socrates?

YESHU: It makes no difference. The kind of loyalty you want I give only to Adonai.

NICK: And what has Adonai ever done for you?

YESHU: Enough to make it possible for me to tell you to get lost, to get out of my sight. Anyone who needs people like Herod and Augustus to do his work will have to get his work done without me. Good-bye, Nick, and I do thank you. You have helped me find out who I am. If I never do anything but set you and your enterprises back I will have lived a good life.

NICK: Nobody talks to me like that. We will meet
                 again, Yeshu, and it will not be a pleasant
                 meeting for you.

He strides away and disappears as quickly as he had appeared. Yeshu remains seated, gazing at the mountains to the east. He sits for some minutes, then reflects:

YESHU: So I have met the Evil One.

He reflects a few minutes. Then he speaks again:

YESHU: It's a funny thing, he seemed just like anyone else. Really a rather charming fellow.

After a few minutes he speaks again:

YESHU: He is far more dangerous than I thought.

I. THE ADVERSARIES

*Two loves have built two cities: the
love of self unto the contempt of God
has built the city of man, and the love
of God unto the contempt of self has
built the city of God.*

—Augustine, *The City of God.*

A. WESTERN CIVILIZATION

I SPEAK of identifying western civilization rather than
defining it. One can hardly proceed through genus and
species; western civilization is unique in its species. The
late Arnold Toynbee distinguished twenty-four (or twenty-
six) different civilizations which can be found in history. It
will be clear that I understand that western civilization has
swallowed and destroyed as individual realities almost all
of these earlier civilizations and is now, unless its progress
is arrested, engaged in swallowing up the few which can
still claim a distinct identity. It is this total assimilative
ability on which I base my observation that it is unique;
given time, it destroys whatever it touches.

There are books, usually of encyclopedic dimensions,
under such titles as the history of western civilization or the
history of European civilization to justify my use of a designation which might seem to be so broad as to be meaningless. I do not know how a Chinese or a Japanese or an
Indian might respond to my choice of a title—probably
with a somewhat hostile reception. The Arab civilization
has for so long been entangled with European civilization
that for my purposes the hopeless task of sorting them out

may be omitted. For this reason I choose the term "western" rather than the term "European." It is, I think, safe to say that the continents of Africa, the Americas and Australia have no surviving indigenous civilizations; they have become western or they remain primitive. The older civilizations will have to prove that they can resist the combination of blandishment and violence which has enabled western civilization to engulf all the cultures which it has hitherto encountered. When I first visited the Near East and saw the flourishing businesses advertising such products as Coca-Cola and Esso (in Arabic letters) and Hollywood movies, I had no doubt about who was winning the cultural battle. I also felt that for the first time I understood what "Hellenism" had been. This is not a value judgment.

Western civilization is a continuous historical phenomenon which has preserved written records in some regions which go back to roughly 3000 B.C. In view of what I said in my preface and what I shall say in other chapters it should be clear that I think the growing use of B.C.E. (before the common era) and C.E. (the common era) is as much (or more) of an implicit theological judgment as the use of the older B.C. (before Christ) and A.D. (anno Domini), since I read it as an attempt to trivialize the meaning of Jesus in history. The enterprise which we call western civilization may be described as a concerted effort to improve the human condition by submitting materials and, as far as technology permits, the forces of nature to the service of human well-being, and the unification of men and women in this purpose by the imposition of discipline administered by some human authority. We could go into more detail, but for my purpose we need not. From the earliest records western civilization has been distinguished from tribal society and the agricultural village by more intense and more widespread social organization. I think so far I have stated nothing but the obvious.

The written record of the continuous growth of civilization begin in the Middle East and in Egypt and spreads from these two centers through the entire Middle East and then to the Mediterranean basin. From there it spreads over the entire continent of Europe and then, having become definitely and irrevocably European, it spreads to the two Americas, Australia and Africa. Finally it moves to the equally old civilizations of the Far East, which it had encountered through Alexander the Great, trade exchanges and the Portuguese, British and Dutch conquests in India and its neighbors. I have left out the Arabic civilization because it refused to become merged with Christendom, a designation (rather a misnomer) created by Europeans for themselves. But I think it not unfair to say that western civilization has achieved domination over Arabic civilization.

These generalities are distressing to a historian, I know; but I am obliged to state what I mean by western civilization and to hope that my readers are persuaded that the term can be used meaningfully. I have treated Arabic civilization as a once powerful rival, now a dominated subject which is doing its best to become western. So far it seems that the same thing is happening to the long independent civilizations of the Far East. The civilization which came into being in the alluvial valleys of the Euphrates and the Nile has changed sites, languages and ethnic composition, but not its character. I run the risk of having this conception designated as poetic and mythological. In the minds of the managers of this civilization it represents mankind advancing to the fullness of the potential of human existence. What mankind still lacks these managers do not believe it will acquire or learn from China, India, Japan—or from the archaic wisdom of its own household stores as expressed by the writers of ancient Greece, Rome, Israel or Mesopotamia. These writers are no longer found in the educational curriculum. It is, I think, an article of modern faith, and perhaps the only article, that humanity reaches its fulfilment only by becoming thoroughly western in its thought patterns, its science and its technology. I did not intend at this point to express value judgments; the rest of the book will have enough of those. But it seems necessary to identify a world of thought and manners, of knowledge and of achievement, which can be easily recognized as distinctively itself.

Robert Nisbet has recently identified five major premises to the idea of progress which are close enough to my attempt to describe some of our presuppositions in western civilization for me to quote them:

> There are at least five major premises to be found in the idea's [the idea of progress] history from the Greeks to our day: belief in the value of the past; conviction of the nobility, even superiority of western civilization; acceptance of the worth of economic and technological growth; faith in reason and in the kind of scientific and scholarly knowledge that can come from reason alone; and, finally, belief in the intrinsic importance, the ineffaceable *worth* of life on this earth. Each of these premises has been severely challenged by doubt and disillusionment, even downright hostility, in the twentieth century, especially the second half.[1]

Hence in laying down character traits it is necessary to state that the most distinctive trait of western civilization escapes a single word, but it cannot escape several. It is dominant, aggressive, acquisitive, arrogant and ruthless. It destroys what does not surrender; it has no mercy on those whom it thinks place an obstacle to its progress. And please do not adduce such legendary figures as Genghis Khan or Tamerlane; these are no longer even bogeymen with whom to frighten children. What enduring traces have these two examples of "The Yellow Peril" left of their passage? They were wiped out by The White Peril. If the Sioux or the Cherokees or the Zulus had been offered a choice, I think they would have chosen Genghis Khan rather than what did hit them. That western civilization has spread farther and endured longer than any competitor was not due solely to the perceived excellence of its wisdom and of its arts and crafts.

One will ask—I have asked myself—what this way of stating the problem adds to such universally admitted generalities as those about the weakness or the corruption of human nature, or the sins of society; or whether my net is cast so wide in time and space that it is in danger of becoming meaningless; or whether I mean by speaking of western civilization to exclude Asian and African civilizations as archaic and untouched by the questions I raise about western civilization. Let me deal with these questions in general now; they are somewhat interlaced and will recur in the subsequent treatment of various topics. By speaking about western civilization, which is an existing concrete historical reality located in a definite time and space, I mean to escape those broad generalities which do not go beyond "sin" and "the human condition." I also intend to speak of "Man" or "humanity" as man or humanity is known to me by my experience. Western civilized humanity is a reality with which I have lived all my life; the drivers and movers of this civilization are predominantly white male

Caucasians of European extraction or those who have identified themselves with the predominant group. It is a human community whose language I speak, which has taught me all I know, with which I have a strange love-hate relationship, which I take for granted, which I cannot leave and which I have no desire to escape. It has made me what I am by establishing the possibilities and the limits of personal development. I think any reader must recognize his or her own membership in that same human community, a community to which Asians and Africans do not belong. I am not addressing their problems; they are capable of doing that themselves. If western civilization is one of their problems, as I suspect it is, they must address it in their own way.

When I speak of this concrete human community, I do not mean to take refuge in such shallow evasions as the sins or the guilt of society. The beauty of such evasions is that no one is expected to do anything about them and that we must just live tolerantly with them. To borrow a popular phrase from fifty years ago, "Relax and enjoy it." It is frequently said of criminals such as thieves or murderers that society and not they is at fault for their crimes. Society (or "the system") indeed exhibits sin and guilt; the purpose of this book is to smear as much of it as I can on the individual members of society, arrogant as this may sound. But most members of society are not thieves or murderers, and they know this. I would like them to think about the sins which they do not recognize as sins, against which there is no law. What I think I hear beneath the indictment of society is that no one is guilty; it is something like the adage that everybody's business is nobody's business. Since we are all guilty, no one in particular need feel responsible or under any obligation. I shall try to set forth what I see as some of the sins of society and attempt to assess the share of guilt which individual members of the society must bear. In at least some of the examples which I shall adduce I have not read anything pertinent from those who are most vocal about the sins of society.

At this preliminary point in my exposition I must plead for the reader's forbearance to see whether I can verify my assertion that I shall be as definite as I know how to be in identifying particular features, recognizable as western, which are not merely examples of sin in general or of inevitable human weakness or corruption. Pelagius was declared a heretic by the Church fifteen hundred years ago for saying more or less than that human weakness and corruption are not inevitable. Like all heretics, he touched on something. When one descends upon some particular weakness or corruption, one finds not only that it was "-evitable," to coin a barbarism, but that human beings, individually or more frequently in concert with other human beings, planned and chose to be weak or corrupt.

Because I am not as familiar with Asian and African civilizations as I think I am with the one in which I have lived more than seventy years, I draw no examples from their experience. I will say that as civilizations they have never encountered Jesus Christ, and therefore they are not open to what I say about western civilization. They have encountered a historic reality called Christendom. I suppose the thesis I am defending could be stated in terms of my fictitious dialogue; when Asia and Africa and the Americas encountered Christendom, it was not Yeshu but Old Nick whom they encountered. I believe it was Thomas B. Costain in one of his novels who describes some Spaniards returning to an early settlement in the West Indies. Discerning some gallows recently put to use on the shore, one Spaniard says to a comrade, "Thank God we are back in a Christian country." Heavy-handed, perhaps, but not essentially distorted.

I am trying to make western civilization the Adversary (for which the Hebrew word is *Satan*). As the exposition proceeds, my right to make this broad accusation will be strengthened, or the accusation will grow so topheavy that it will collapse of itself into unreason. One may wonder—and I think that no one will take this as a jest—whether western civilization itself may collapse before my arguments do. It is hardly a rewarding task to attempt an analysis of a terminal disease which may be so far advanced that death will supervene before the analysis is completed. Hence I have to say that I hope I am wrong.

B. CHRISTIANITY

If I say simply that I am trying to establish an essential and irreconcilable opposition between western civilization and Christianity, I am more likely to be shot down for intolerable vagueness for the use of the second term of my pair than for the use of the first. As soon as one asks the question, "What is Christianity?", one realizes that an answer seems impossible; one can never formulate a statement upon which all Christians will agree. And this impossibility seems to abort any discourse of the sort I am attempting to mount here. And since I believe that it is absolutely necessary to mount some such discourse, I am compelled to attack the impossible, thinking that if I succeed in identifying "Christianity" in some passably intelligible way, I shall have gone most of the distance towards establishing the opposition of which I speak.

Christianity in general signifies a set of religious beliefs, observances and practices which is well enough known to be distinguished without much thought from non-Christian religions. Judaism, Islam, Buddhism and Hinduism may be taken as obvious examples of four old and well established religions which insist that they are not Christian, and which have millions of adherents. If one were to ask, "What is a Christian?", the answer might seem to be equally impossible. This would not keep several hundred millions of people from answering "Christian" if they were asked their religion. Many of these millions profess readiness to die for this affirmation, as many have done before them. Surely, one would think, professed readiness to die a violent death to assert a religious confession would seem to imply that the confessor knows what the confession means. Yet I cannot accomplish my task by saying that Christianity is that complex of beliefs for which Christians say they are ready to die; we still would not know what those beliefs are. Many Christians might say, as many of their predecessors have said, that Christianity is that complex of beliefs for which they are willing to kill; and this complicates the question so much as to demand further examination, to be taken up later. I shall say now that readiness to kill for one's beliefs, however orthodox they may be, is essentially unchristian.

When one looks at the hundreds of churches and creeds which call themselves Christian and are accepted as Christian by other dissenting bodies, one may with reason wonder whether there is really a Christian creed, or whether, if one were devised, it would hardly differ from a creed of sincere and benevolent humanism. It seems fairly well established that the churches themselves are the main reason why many intelligent modern men and women do not call themselves Christian. Certainly such an artificially devised non-sectarian creed would be accepted as a profession of faith by no Christian church. For hundreds of years these Christian churches have disputed with each other, and often they have literally warred with each other. I cannot resist remarking that while modern civilized societies no longer think that differences of religious belief are worth fighting and killing, modern civilized societies have found no lack of other causes for which to fight and kill. This seems to suggest that modern western Man, my anti-hero, does not think that religious belief is worth killing for, but an unfavorable trade balance is. But let us not be distracted. Profession of Christianity has always meant historically profession of membership in a church. Either all the churches believe the same thing, and the differences are mere idle and somewhat expensive sectarianism, or they do not believe the same thing, and we are back at my question: what is Christianity, and what is a Christian?

Let me repeat what I said above; I am a member and a minister in good standing (at least so far) of a major Christian church. What I think I know about Christianity I have learned mostly from my membership in that church. A rather militant Lutheran layman, a church officer, once said at a meeting where I was in attendance that the Catholic Church was not a very good place to learn what Christianity is. This encounter suggested that members of most Christian churches have to say the same thing to justify their membership in their own church. I do not think I can find any "genuine" Christianity by departing from the historic Christian community, any more than I can find genuine "humanity" by withdrawing from the human community of western civilization. Hence what I am about to say is in no way to be taken as suggesting that I am moving towards a perfect abstraction of Christianity, a sort of Platonic essence existing only in the world of ideas. I fear "real" Christianity at its best is imperfect, that Christians often cease to think like Christians and to act like Christians; but there is something from which most of them, possibly all of them, know that they are deviating. That something is the historic reality of Jesus.

In writing "the historic reality of Jesus" I realize that I have written something on which not all modern Christian scholars, much less all Christians, are in agreement. My esteemed colleague, Pheme Perkins, has written in a review of some recent books on introduction to the New Testament:

> The disappearance of genuine philosophical and theological questions from the modern university may also be allied with the disappearance of Jesus from New Testament introductions. Perrin-Duling [the authors of one of the books under review] is the most explicit example. Discussion of Jesus is relegated to the final chapter. Jesus is the presupposition of there being a New Testament, but New Testament study is *not about Jesus* [italics by Perkins]. It is about the history and literary remains of the early Christian movement, which held various beliefs about Jesus. Koester [another author under review] is equally short on the question. The vast syncretism of the Hellenistic world, which he deals with in his first volume, leads to a portrayal of Christianity as one among the many Hellenistic cults.[2]

Dr. Perkins is harsh in her criticism, but I do not think she is unfair; in fact, I think it has long been high time for some one as academically qualified as Dr. Perkins to say something like this. One would like to know how Dr.

Koester, a professor at Harvard's Divinity School (the *alma mater* of Dr. Perkins) or the late Norman Perrin would explain why the interest in their academic departments and their books and lectures is so much greater than the interest generated by the departments which study the cults of Cybeie, Isis and Mithra, if it were not for the person whom Perrin and his continuator, Duling, relegated to the last chapter. In contemporary New Testament scholarship no one carries on the insanity of a German scholar named Drews and one or two others of the early twentieth century, who claimed that Jesus never existed. For my contemporaries Jesus is not the Great Non-Existent or the Great Mythic Hero; but he is perilously close to becoming the Great Unknown, and that is only a short step from becoming the Great Irrelevant.

See where one phrase has led me. Let me resume that if, instead of "the historical reality of Jesus," I write simply "Jesus" as that something from which Christians know they are deviating, the phrase will pass. We can postpone the question of who or what is Jesus. I do not know how many of my colleagues would accept my statement of my own beliefs made in the preface. I am sure some would say that I believe more than I can justify, others that I fall below a minimum which Christian belief requires. But it is obvious that my own statement of belief can be no more than a personal fantasy if Jesus is the Great Unknown, or worse, the Great Irrelevant. I have to say what Dr. Perkins was too polite to say except by implication, that a massive introduction to the New Testament which squeezes the *raison d'etre* of the New Testament into a single final chapter is more than a colossal failure; it denies that Jesus is of any importance either for understanding the New Testament or for understanding life.

Hence I propose that the Jesus whom Christians of any denomination profess to be the figure of supreme importance in religion is known only through the New Testament. All Christians accord a respect to these books as sources which they do not accord to Christian art and literature, which have produced so much devotional Jesus fiction. The New Testament may be the one thing which all Christian denominations have in common. This does not mean that they understand it or use it very much. I am going to write this book on several assumptions which my colleagues—Jesus love them—may reject, and I must say I do not care. I assume that the New Testament is not a mystery wrapped in a riddle and enveloped in an enigma, to reconstruct a phrase stolen from a recent over-rated wordsmith. I am aware of the problems in ascertaining what Jesus actually said, but I am not going to be trapped in the illusions of the "exact words" or the "authentic words." I do not worship the text, and I think I shall have enough examples of irreverence to scandalize the devout. At the same time, I think it is an idle word game to say that because the exact words of Jesus are lost beyond recovery we cannot learn his mind with assurance on any topic, that we just do not know what he stood for. There is a general drift to the New Testament which it takes a lot of erudition to miss. To illustrate, no one remembered or attributed to Jesus any sayings on how to acquire and accumulate wealth, or how to acquire and administer power over others, or how to conduct armed hostilities, private or public. One may make too much of this; historically Christians (with rare exceptions) have made nothing of it.

I am going to assume that Jesus did not found a sect or a school (or a church, if you wish). He seems to have taken no care that his words be preserved or organized into a

doctrine. The earliest designation of what he began was a
"way," and his disciples felt that that way should be preserved. I am going to assume that Jesus, a Palestinian
villager who spoke almost exclusively to his own kind,
generally couched his words in language which was within
the reach of anyone who had reached the mental age of
twelve; I understand the sophisticated arts of television are
addressed to the same mental level. This does not mean
that those who remembered and transmitted his words did
not add subtleties and refinements, sometimes adolescent,
which they did not hear from him.

I believe Jesus was unique; but over the years I think I
have learned to understand him better if I think of
Abraham Lincoln, another unlettered villager who could
speak with power, lucidity and profundity. Both Jesus
and Lincoln spoke from a fund of folk wisdom which Lincoln did not learn from Harvard, nor Jesus from the
scribes. A man from Harvard gave another and quite
forgettable address at Gettysburg on November 20, 1863;
it lasted two hours and was reported in full by the *New
York Times,* which, with its unerring nose for news,
reported that "Mr. Lincoln also spoke." The people
whom Jesus addressed did not ask what he meant; they
said, "Right on," or whatever Aramaic phrase expresses
it, or "I don't believe it," and walked away. I shall not
waste your time and mine explaining at great length (it
usually takes great length) that Jesus did not really mean
what he said, but something else already said so often that
it has long been conventional wisdom. Far more books
have already been written which do that much better than I
can or want to.

This may suggest that what I have in mind is to lay down
a charter for a new church of the Gospel or of the New

Testament—to do what Martin Luther, John Calvin and a host of others have already done, with what success I leave to others to judge. I repeat that I have no intention of departing from the Roman Catholic confession I embrace. This does not mean that I accept the Roman Catholic confession uncritically, and I think this will become evident. I believe a "church" is a necessary means for an individual person to find and follow the "way" of Jesus in the particular time, place and world in which the person lives. I do not believe that Jesus showed a "way" in which to escape from the world of people. The "way" is not a solitary adventure which ends in communion with the deity. The "way" is to be found and followed in the company of one's fellows. A church can and ought to interpret this way in the reality of social life. If one were to attempt to sum up what Jesus is reported as saying in the New Testament, an inadequate but not the worst summary ever devised would be directions on how to live at peace with one's fellows.

For various reasons a church can here and there fail in its task of contemporary interpretation, mostly because of pressure from the world in which it lives to adapt its interpretation to the demands of the world, because of excessive attachment to its past teachings, because of insensitivity to present needs and problems, and other such things. I shall return to these hindrances to a living interpretation of the "way" in a number of subsequent passages. I do not say that this is all a church has to do; but if it does not do this, it fails in an essential duty both to its members and to him whose name it proudly wears. There is no church, including my own, which does not have have an impressive list of failures in doing this duty, extending right to the present. I am going to try to be specific in dealing with what appear to be some key failures.

II. SALVATION THROUGH WEALTH

Fill the earth and subdue it.

—Genesis 1:28

I ASK my readers to join me in considering some differences in the attitude of Jesus towards wealth, as it is presented in the New Testament, and the prevailing attitude of contemporary culture in western civilization. I say the prevailing attitude; I am not concerned with individual persons or small groups which might justly claim to be exceptions. Likewise I say "presented in the New Testament," aware that a captious critic might interpose that I am entitled to say no more than "it can be deduced from the New Testament." It is indeed part of my exposition to assert clearly that there is no room for such evasions, either in the name of exact scholarship or of anything else. I think the two opposing positions are lucidly clear.

Let me first take up the attitude of contemporary culture, the same attitude which western civilization has maintained since the beginning of recorded history. It seems safe to say that western civilization has exhibited more skill and ingenuity in exploiting the resources of nature for the production of wealth than any other civilization of which we have experience or record. The distribution of wealth so produced is another question to which we must return; but it seems incontestable that the most successful countries in western civilization have made more wealth available to more members of their national communities than humankind has ever experienced before. I risk a value judgment when I say that the pursuit of wealth in this culture is not so much esteemed as the supreme good

51

but as the basic good without which no other good, common or private, can be achieved. I take "wealth" in both sense #5 in *Webster's New Universal Unabridged Dictionary* ("in economics (a) everything having economic value measurable in price; (b) any useful material thing capable of being bought, sold, or stocked for useful disposition") and sense #1 ("much money or property; riches; large possessions of money, goods, or land; great abundance of worldly goods, affluence, opulence"). I do not say that modern civilization denies that there are real goods which cannot be bought, sold, stocked or priced; I do say that our culture believes and often says that it is not possible to achieve these goods without a sufficiency of wealth (useful material things).

A few illustrations come to mind. One I have often expressed in recent years, I suppose because advancing age sharpens some sensitivities while it dulls others: one is as free, meaning as able to resist the imposition of another's will upon one, as one can afford to be. Freedom is certainly an intangible good, but one is a fool if one thinks that it is not bought, sold, stocked or priced. Another illustration appears in Roman Catholic religious communities which are sincerely and genuinely dedicated agents of such intangible goods as education, health care and provisions of kindly services for the indigent and sick. No matter how much dedication their members exhibit, these organizations are helpless without a sufficiency of useful material goods, in spite of the fact that their members as individuals profess poverty. I am quite sure from my own experience that most of these communities do not fall under the alarming statistical law that 71 cents out of every dollar collected for charitable purposes is spent by, for and on the collecting agencies and never reach those for whom the funds are collected.

A third example, offensive only to those who share my destiny of writing books for publication, shows me as a person who pretends to deal with the intangible goods (shall I say such intangibles as beauty, truth and goodness?); I suppose Larry Flynt and Henry Miller feel the same way about what they produce. I know very well that what I pass off as beauty, truth and goodness are marketable goods which can be bought, sold, priced and stocked, and which, even for as obscure a wordsmith as I am, is a means of securing a sufficiency of useful material things, if not a great abundance of them. It is only fair to my fellow wordsmiths to note that the Authors League recently surveyed its members and found that most of them earn $4,500 a years by writing, and make a living by other occupations. The modern civilized western world is not a seller's market for beauty, truth and goodness. I shall return to this topic under another heading.

Whether one likes it or not, one's very membership in western society imprisons one in an ethos which directs most of one's actions even if one does not believe in it. I feel like a passenger on a leaky, sinking ship who may criticize the navigation and maintenance of the craft, the lack of discipline of the crew and the bad manners of the passengers, all with truth and justice; but he has no place to go. If I teach or write, as I have spent my life doing, I teach or write according to the ethos of my culture, to which I have sufficiently well adjusted; and the ethos of successful teaching or writing, or even to remain active in both occupations, is to accept them as small functions in a vast enterprise instituted solely for the acquisition and accumulation of wealth. I could retire to a hermitage near Sedona, Arizona, only because I have saved enough from the market place to abandon the market place. Is money important, or is it the only thing?

Let me think of such basics as love, family, home. I do not know that many people really believe that these cannot be sustained without affluence; but if they do not believe it, the writers of modern advertising must be seriously misunderstanding the minds of their customers. The success of advertisers and of their clients does not indicate that they do misunderstand. Those who bring sons and daughters into the world may think of them as joys and supports in their old age, but they would be wiser to think of their warm and loving Social Security office. Their beautiful little ones they may think of as very soon demanding $60,000 for a college education. If they cannot stand the thought of that, they had better wonder whether it is ethical to think of bringing underprivileged children into the world. This comes perilously close to thinking of children as goods which can be priced, stocked or withheld from the market; no doubt I am in danger of overstating the prevailing pervasive ethos. Perhaps one can have as much paternal and maternal love, like freedom, as we can afford. We have long since reached the point where we can no longer afford filial love.

Health is certainly an intangible good—or is it? Contemporary western society is proud of the fact that it has removed most of the major hazards to health and made medical care available to everyone—everyone, that is, within certain social and economic levels of certain western political communities. We boast that smallpox, syphilis, tuberculosis and cholera—to mention only a few of our notable medical victories—have been removed or at least had their fangs extracted. That this intangible good is neither achieved nor sustained without charges imposed on everyone (which a few generations ago only the wealthy could pay) is obvious to any taxpayer. No wonder they call it the health industry. Like freedom, we get as much health and health care as we can afford.

We seem to forget that the culture has introduced a few hazards to health which did not exist a hundred years ago. I do not know whether it is still statistically validated that the major cause of death for white males under the age of twenty-five is the automobile; for black males of the same age it is murder. Certainly it was not the automobile a hundred years ago; it is probably illuminating (or something else) that figures on the causes of death among young black males were not kept a hundred years ago. I suppose some would call it progress that we now count the corpses. I have no comparative statistics on how many deaths and crippling illnesses occur due to the consumption of illicit drugs now and a century ago. Nor have I any ready statistics on the deaths and injuries due to the automobile set against deaths and injuries on the railroads and horse-drawn vehicles in 1886. I suppose I could find them; if I did, so what? It is idle to boast about our health care systems when we heedlessly kill fifty thousand people and maim two or three times as many in order to pay the price of the personal freedom of unskilled, incompetent and drunken drivers to enjoy their personal transportation. The automobile in our personal lives is an apt symbol of the dedication of our culture to wealth. To lack a car is to be only half alive and not even half free.

It may seem that the dedication of western civilization to wealth is no more than a fulfilment of the biblical injunction to humanity at its creation to fill the earth and subdue it, and to exercise dominion over the fish, the birds and all the living things that move upon the earth (Genesis 1:28). This franchise is attributed to the school of scribes who are called "The Priestly Writer." A somewhat different and less liberal donation is found in the document called "The Yahwist;" before the sin of the man and the woman the scribe says that the Lord set man in the garden to cultivate and care for it, and gave the man freedom to eat all the fruits of the garden except the fruit of knowledge (Genesis 2:16-17). After the sin of the first couple the man is told that the earth is cursed on his account, and that he must eat its produce in pain and sweat (Genesis 3:17-18). Both the Priestly Writer and the Yahwist are dealing with the thought patterns and the language of myth; this does not mean that either of them doubted that he was dealing very seriously with topics of the highest importance. If one wishes to quote either of these myths in support of what humankind has done and is doing to the world of nature, one must notice that two different and opposing views are set forth. One is a view of the unrestrained freedom of humanity to do what it pleases with nature; the other is a view of a nature which constantly resists humanity's effort to dominate it, a resistance which is effectively God's denial of our right to subdue nature to human purposes. One view is just as biblical as the other. If one says that the position of humankind before nature is not a theological question at all, this comes close to saying that human conduct is not a theological question at all. One must then face the question whether there are any restraints upon human freedom to do whatever the human species can do. I shall return to this question.

The basis of western civilization is the amassing of wealth through the exploitation of nature. Except for a few feeble protests from environmentalist groups, this is accepted without question. I have to say that I am not sure how many of these groups really question the principle of the exploitation of nature. I am not sure whether I question it as much as the Yahwist questioned it, or as much as Jesus questioned it, as I hope to show. I sit writing at a machine powered by electricity in a building heated, cooled and illuminated by the same power, fed and clothed by the use of materials made available to me with little or no personal trouble. I and my kind certainly get more out of the accursed soil than thorns and thistles, and I eat bread (or cake, to borrow a phrase from an unfortunate lady) by the sweat of some one else' brow, not my own. Without the exploitation of nature I would sit here as helpless as Job on his dunghill, and about as useless. So why wonder about the sincerity of the Sierra Club? As far as I know, its members enjoy no more of the exploitaiton of nature than I do. Both they and I could stand some self-examination.

I see that this is a problem imposed on me by the civilization of which I am a member and the fruits of whose exploitations I enjoy. I have spent my life, since I became aware that it is a personal problem as well as a cultural problem, convinced (and not really discontented) that there is nothing I can do about it, and therefore that there is nothing I ought to do about it. I shall mention later a few Christians who refused to admit that the problem was too much for them. At least I owe it to myself and to my Christian profession to admit that Jesus is at least credited with a different position about this problem. And when I begin to think about his position, I am reminded of what I said earlier: the sayings of Jesus are couched in language which is accessible to anyone who has reached the mental age of twelve. Subtlety is not depth, and depth is not subtlety; only wits confuse the two, while twelve-year-olds see the difference at once.

Before I approach the sayings of Jesus, I wish to set forth some other elements of our dedication to wealth. It is an essential element in this dedication that what is accepted as the fundamental good, without which the society cannot achieve other goods, is also accepted as the fundamental personal good without which the individual cannot achieve even the intangible goods—wisdom and virtue, for example. Thus the basic social evil is poverty. Any social or personal evil can be eradicated if the society or the individual person can spend enough money. Therefore any other (and lesser evil) must be borne rather than poverty. Let me illustrate from war, a difficult example. No one questions that war is a social and personal evil. One need not be a Marxist to recognize that most wars are fought over the division of wealth; nations and peoples strive for a larger share of an amount of wealth which is not regarded as enough to go around or which would be unduly diminished by sharing with others. Is war so bad? It depends on the loot. Would war cease if there were no international quarrels about wealth? I do not think so; this will come up under another heading. But as I said earlier, western civilized people have always regarded wealth as a legitimate cause for fighting and killing. I believe it is safe to generalize conventional wisdom as expressing or implying that international peace can be achieved only by the enrichment of the impoverished nations and peoples; that is, peace too can be bought, sold, priced and stocked.

No doubt this will be dismissed as a vast over-simplification of very complex political and economic processes. It will be said that while Jesus may have put his wisdom within the reach of twelve-year-olds, the causes of war and the construction of peace demand a higher degree of sophisticated intelligence and learning. I suppose it would be snide of me to say that so far, especially in the last eighty years, these complex processes have totally eluded the grasp of those endowed with high levels of sophisticated intelligence and learning. It seems to me that to reserve these questions for an elite corps of experts (proved by their record to be incompetent) is to say that most of the men and women who suffer and die in wars they did not start and would not support if they had a choice are incapable of grasping the issues at stake. This could be dismissed as snobbism, did it not touch so many people so closely. They are the people whom Jesus declared blessed, possibly because they are not in a position to make decisions which would deprive large numbers of their peers of life and welfare in the name of abstractions which exceed the capacity of their twelve-year-old minds, or for the acquisition of wealth which they will never share. A Roman poet named Horace (actually Quintus Horatius Flaccus), who hired out a genuinely brilliant talent to become a political hack for Augustus, in one of his better moments wrote: *Quidquid delirant reges, plectuntur Achivi*. I paraphrase, with less skill than Horace: whenever politicians go crazy, it is the poor taxpayers who get clobbered.

Let us admit that conventional wisdom will not allow me to discuss war on the simple basis that someone has something which someone else wants, and let us turn to the fundamental value of wealth for the individual person and family. Here we encounter the basic social gospel of contemporary thought: there is nothing wrong with the individual members of society or with the internal structure of any single political society which cannot be set right by an equitable distribution of wealth. This puts it crudely because it is basically crude thinking. Such details as what is an equitable distribution of wealth are mere details which can be left to the planners to be worked out in practice. Crime will cease when the poor have adequate food, clothing and housing, and when ignorance is eradicated by a full system of public education specializing in computer skills. Elsewhere in this book I try to make it clear that I make no plea for the kind of exploitation which makes wealth by producing and sustaining slums; and I hope this entitles me to say that it has never been proved that crime is committed only by the destitute—in fact, my unscholarly impression is that most crime, like most of everything, is committed by the middle class. Crime is an amateur effort to redistribute the wealth—to do more directly and more cheaply what the social engineers try and fail to do by an expensive, cumbersome and slow bureaucracy. I think it is safe to say that social engineers demand and get the power to dispose of sums of money which make the Rockefellers, the Duponts, the Mellons and the Kennedys look like small potatoes. And the management of these vast sums, like the management of the enterprises associated with the names just mentioned, is an occupation which frees those who engage in it from poverty for the rest of their lives. Am I suggesting that social planning is a kind of sophisticated white-collar crime? By no means; I am suggesting that it is a way of enriching oneself by the use of other people's money without their consent.

That the redistribution of wealth according to the standards set up by experts (who do not themselves live like Trappists) will achieve all that is promised is an assumption based on the belief that social values, like the other intangible goods mentioned (such as peace, freedom and love), can be bought, sold, priced and stocked. This assumption awaits demonstration, and it is plain that it can never be demonstrated. If wealth assures happiness and goodness, why are the rich regarded as anti-social moral lepers, a class fit only for extermination? The assumption is proposed as a way of life and a way of government which is always in movement towards the promised objective, which is never attained. I will be thought facetious and trivial if I say that Louis XVI could have kept his throne and his head if, like Henri IV, he had promised a chicken in every pot on Sunday. Henri IV, of course, was assassinated, but not, I think, for promising a richer diet. I do not care whether I am thought facetious or trivial or not. The redistribution of income as planned by social experts is not the Reign of God, and it approaches blasphemy to say that it is. I know that no one says this. Most people do not say it because they believe that the Reign of God lies geographically adjacent to Utopia and the Land of Oz, others because they think that the Reign of God is actually a theological name for the Reign of Humanity, built by the achievements of men and women.

When we consider the exploitation of nature, we must not omit one of the earliest forms of this exploitation and the most enduring; I mean that resource which nature furnishes most generously, even prodigally, and whose exploitation requires no more than the most primitive technology. I mean the exploitation of the human person. I remember reading about thirty or forty years ago that the Soviet Union had to be interested in India because India had one of the largest pools of cheap, unskilled labor in the world. The writer did not say, as I remember it, that this was the reason why the British Crown had so long been interested in India, so I think I may venture to add it on my own. Real wealth (opulence) is now what it has always been, an unlimited amount of people to do your work for you at wages which are high enough to keep them alive and working, and low enough to keep them too tired and hungry to get ambitious. The few who preserve their ambition are easily coopted into the system of ownership and management. The barbed wire millionaire, John W. Gates, not an unusually perceptive example of a robber baron, is credited with the statement that he could hire half the working class to kill the other half any time he needed. Was he right? He assumed that the workers were motivated by the same motives as himself. He expressed an insight possessed by all who have exploited people, the insight that the help which they needed to exploit people could be obtained by promising to a sufficient but limited number of people a share of the profits.

I believe that we still do not know how the Pyramids were built; we know that they were the work of a vast pool of unskilled forced labor. The modern entrepreneur would like to know how this vast pool was brought to submission. I suspect modern entrepreneurs have little to learn from the Pharaohs about bringing large masses of cheap unskilled labor into submission. The western world did not rid itself of slavery until the nineteenth century, and the last nation to accept the abolition of slavery was that nation which not long afterwards accepted a gift from another nation of a gigantic female figure symbolizing the liberty which the receiving nation had rather tardily proclaimed. When this statue was erected that nation had not finished its task of exterminating the culture of Native Americans, which of necessity involved the extermination of enough Native Americans to make the entire nation secure for European immigrants.

Why did not the European immigrants enslave the Native Americans, as they had enslaved Africans brought to America by slave traders? Millions of Africans (the estimates of the numbers are uncertain) were brought out of Africa to work the plantations in semi-tropical and tropical climates which even the planters would have thought inhuman to force European workers to tolerate. And it was inhuman, but European wise men had discovered that Africans were not really human. The Native Americans were not submissive enough to make good slaves; this is not to say that Africans were, but they had been deprived of their roots, as one of their descendants has recently and poignantly shown. The Assyrians (who were ahead of their time in business and politics) discovered in the ninth century B.C. that nothing destroys a people's self-awareness and turns them into docile subjects and workers like transporting them *en masse* from the land of their nativity. The Native Americans were really too few to enslave but too numerous to be transported, and where could they have been taken? Transportation to reservations had been tried early in the nineteenth century when there seemed to be unlimited square miles of useless land; but by 1880 it had become clear that European immigrants needed the whole country, nothing less. It was easier to maintain a military operation and let battles, the destruction of wildlife, the onset of diseases (most of them imported from Europe), malnutrition and intoxication do their work in removing the last obstacle to the creation of a land of the free and a home of the brave. The Assyrians would have admired and envied this work of pacification accomplished at so little expense in twenty-five years.

I have passed rather quickly over the Native Americans because they were not exploited; they were rather an obstacle to progress and they were removed. As an example of how western civilization deals with those who do not readily submit to progress the Native American will come up again. My purpose was simply to set forth some reasons why this human resource was not exploited; the reasons are not flattering either to the Christian morality or the elementary human decency of our ancestors. Karl Marx, to whom I do not often appeal, has documented the exploitation of the rural English population and the inhabitants of the nineteenth century English slums to all satisfaction. No doubt similar evidence has been collected for other European countries which I have not seen. Americans know or can learn how their own cities and industries grew from nothing to the world's leading industrial nation—a position now, I believe, under threat. This topic will come up for discussion again. I think Marx's statistics are well enough known to excuse me from quoting them at length, and it would take length. I content myself with a quotation in which he targets some of the conventional excuses for the industrial exploitation of persons; the reader of Marx becomes accustomed to the absence of basic civility in his prose:

> . . . the Church of England parson, Townsend, glorified misery as a necessary condition of wealth. "Legal constraint (to labour) is attended with too much trouble, violence and noise. . . Whereas hunger is not only a peaceable, silent and unremitted pressure, but as the most natural motive to industry and labour it calls forth the most powerful exertions." Everything therefore depends upon making hunger permanent among the working-class, and for this, according to Townsend, the principle of population, especially active among the poor, provides. "It seems to be a law of nature that the poor should be to a certain degree improvident [i.e., so improvident as to be born without a silver spoon in the mouth], that there may always be some to fulfil the most servile, the most sordid, and the most ignoble offices in the community. The stock of human happiness

is thereby much increased, whilst the most delicate are not only relieved from drudgery...but are left at liberty to pursue those callings which are suited to their various dispositions...it [the Poor Law] tends to destroy the harmony and beauty, the symmetry and order of that system which God and Nature have established in the world." If the Venetian monk found in the fatal destiny that makes misery eternal, the *raison d'etre* of Christian charity, celibacy, monasteries and holy houses, the Protestant prebendary finds in it a pretext for condemning the laws in virtue of which the poor possess a right to a miserable public relief.

"The progress of social wealth," says Storch, "begins this useful class of society...which performs the most wearisome, the vilest, the most disgusting functions, which takes, in a word, on its shoulders all that is disagreeable and servile in life, and procures thus for other classes leisure, serenity of mind and conventional [c'est bon!] dignity of character.[1]

Whatever be the fruits of the Industrial Revolution and, at least in the United States, an unprecedented wide distribution of the wealth produced, the whole thing is subject to the remark of John L Lewis: "There is blood on that coal." There is blood on everything we buy, sell, use and consume. Without the exploitation of people, the exploitation of other natural resources is impossible. When I was born, fresh fruit and vegetables were rare luxuries available only to the rich. They are now available to the middle-class—or is the middle class the *nouveaux riches,* Dives dining sumptuously while Lazarus picks his fruit and vegetables? By chance I was given an opportunity to visit and lecture in East Africa (the three countries which were formerly British East Africa) and see how some of my coffee was picked. Quite certainly the fruit, vegetables and coffee are no longer restricted to the rich; but if we paid the pickers enough to live as decently as we do, we would think we could not afford the coffee. In Africa a healthy young adult male cannot possibly make more than $1.50 a day picking coffee. It is no wonder the women and children are compelled by that strange force of hunger (mentioned by one of Marx's sources) to share in the picking. As long as I am offered these items which are smeared with the blood of those who pick them, I am deaf to the social engineers and their plans for a richer (and therefore better) world, because I think they are as phony as a three-dollar bill. Having retired in California, I am sometimes a bit unreasonably and superstitiously apprehensive because of my very proximity to the San Joaquin and Imperial Valleys. It is something like living in the neighborhood of Sodom and Gomorrah. But God really does not do things that way, does he?

Remove the element of human exploitation from the history of western civilization, and how much "progress," meaning the accumulation and diffusion of wealth, would be left? We would be scratching for nuts and berries, living in caves, and wearing the skins of dead animals. It runs all the way from the peasants of ancient Egypt who built the Pyramids and tilled the fields by forced labor to the produce pickers of the United States. Child labor is as old as children and as recent as this morning's groceries. Exploitation runs through the mines of the ancient Egyptians in the intolerable climate of the Sinai peninsula (digging for jewelry, for God's sake) to the modern coal mines of Europe and America and the gold and diamond mines of Africa.

I am not touching on many of the lurid details which can be found by a close look at the history of the exploitation of nature and of human beings, such as the innumerable wars in which the principal booty was captives for the slave markets, the plantations of ancient Rome and of recent America, the slave markets such as Delos (which at its peak handled 12,000 slaves a day) or Cartagena. I suggest as a point for inquiry and not a point of dispute that the whole fabric of western civilization is so totally interwoven with the need for cheap unskilled labor that it cannot survive without this element, and that civilization shows no signs of any serious effort to eliminate this feature from its composition. The sector of American labor which is growing most rapidly is the service industries. There is a certain amount of dirty work that must be done to sustain the fabric of civilized living which no one is going to do unless they are forced by some compulsion (maybe the fear of starvation) that it does not appear how forced labor can be abolished. Civilized living might be roughly defined as the skill of living without doing the dirty work and of getting someone else to do it. Western men and women have not yet shown the ability to sustain their standard of living without leaning upon some depressed class. Jesus is quoted as saying that the poor you have always with you. If we do not have them, we will make them, because we need them absolutely.

III. PERDITION THROUGH WEALTH

*What does it profit a man who gains
the whole world—and destroys
himself?*

—Mark 8:36.

HERE as elsewhere we must be aware of the dangers in proposing anything as the "teaching of Jesus." The Gospels contain no teaching of Jesus; they give us collections of scattered and often disjointed sayings. These sayings can be arranged under headings, topics or themes; but conclusions which can be drawn from such arrangements are the teaching not of Jesus but of his interpreters. This does not imply that such conclusions cannot be legitimate; indeed, they can be irresistible. But one is aware of venerable "doctrines" proposed as the teaching of Jesus, such as the primacy and infallibility of the Roman Pontiff, the establishment of the monarchical episcopate and the apostolic succession, none of which has the slightest foundation in the sayings of Jesus, and one takes due precautions. The sayings attributed to Jesus can, with varying degrees of probability, be traced back to the words of Jesus himself; sayings so traced are called by my colleagues "authentic" sayings. Sayings not judged authentic are attributed to the early disciples and scribes who made efforts to reconstruct the sayings of Jesus by the use of imagination or to construct what they thought he would have said about situations concerning which the collective memory of the disciples preserved no authentic sayings.

The judgment of how faithful these collected sayings are to the historical Jesus is an area of theological warfare which has been carried on for nearly two centuries. If I had to reach assured and generally accepted conclusions about these controverted questions, I should not attempt to write this book. I assume that the "real" or the "historical" Jesus is more responsible than anyone else for what is preserved of his sayings and his doings in the Gospels. I do not believe that the Jesus of the Gospels is the creation of the nameless and barely literate believers of the first century. To identify this Jesus as a "teacher" is to give him a role which Paul, the earliest literate Christian who has left us a written statement of his belief, did not recognize Jesus as fulfilling. The Jesus of the Gospels did not exist when Paul wrote his letters. Yet Paul and the authors of the Gospels believed in the same Jesus, unless one wishes to run the real danger of saying that what Jesus was and said is lost beyond recovery, and is therefore irrelevant to modern Christian belief. I prefer to accept other risks inherent in my approach; these, after all, can be corrected if there is some base to which one can return after flight in the wrong direction.

That base I find in the Jesus of the Gospels, elusive as he is and misunderstood by the Evangelists as he was and distorted by his interpreters as he has been. If by these various processes he has been lost to posterity, we might as well give up trying to find meaning in a Christian view of life and turn the effort to the cultivation of Mammon, to use a phrase attributed to him. My contemporaries call it secularism. I find the Jesus of the Gospels, with all the obstacles to a clear vision of him, credible, more credible than the substitutes proposed, and I cannot say why. Some things you have to believe. I hope this makes it clear that I find necessity and ample room for intelligent and free discussion of the criticism and the interpretation of the Gospels. I have long recognized that to refuse to accept these discussions is to accept the certainty of self-imprisonment in the bondage of refusal to think and refusal to learn.

Obviously this topic could receive a book-length treatment, and the topic has received such treatment; for this is the topic of hermeneutics. I do not want to get stalled on this topic because my experience of the topic and of my colleagues is that they spend so much time worrying how to interpret that they forget the task of interpreting. I want to see whether I can make some sense out of what Jesus might have said or done to help me to find a Christian way to survive spiritually in a world which seems totally dedicated to make such survival impossible. I can no longer wait to see whether Gadamer or Ricoeur or Merleau-Ponty will tell me how to think about it; damn it, I am a big boy now. So I shall run the risk of trying to find out whether Jesus—or what the earliest records of what Jesus said and did, bad as my colleagues seem to think they are—can tell me how to think about it. I think I have earned the right to escape classification as a fundamentalist; certainly the fundamentalists of my acquaintance do not think I am one of them, and if I finish this book they will be sure I am not.

Before we attack either the authenticity or the interpretation of particular sayings, I think we can accept a general statement that the sayings of Jesus exhibit sympathy with the poor and with poverty and hostility towards the wealthy and wealth. Let me say that if remarks about women were attributed to Jesus like the remarks about the wealthy attributed to him, the feminist movement would want to abolish both him and the Gospels. We may find some of this attitude summed up in the saying twice attributed to Jesus, "You cannot serve two masters; you cannot serve God and Mammon" (Matthew 6:24; Luke

16:13). We can at once face the question whether this saying is original with Jesus or may be a commonplace proverb which he quoted to express his own mind or which the Gospel scribe quoted as expressing the mind of Jesus. If this saying fits the general attitude of Jesus toward wealth and poverty as expressed above, then it is a trivial concern whether the saying is the exact words of Jesus (probably not) or was thought by the scribe to express the thinking of Jesus on the topic (it certainly does). The texts to be reviewed in this chapter do support the summary of his attitude which I have suggested.

We find, whenever Jesus says something which runs directly counter to conventional assumptions, that reasons are at once found to question the "authenticity" of the saying or the meaning of the words. This is a piece of hermeneutics which I offer the reader quite gratuitously. Norman Perrin once wrote that a saying of Jesus which cannot be run back to biblical wisdom or rabbinical wisdom or Hellenistic wisdom is very probably authentic. This does not mean that everything Jesus said was a departure from some conventional pattern. Jesus could quote cliches, as we all do; but we are not remembered for quoting cliches.

For the point now under discussion it may be admitted that the attitude toward wealth and poverty summed up above is not a total departure from biblical, rabbinical or Hellenistic wisdom. For this reason I left open the possibility that Jesus was quoting an existing proverb which has not been traced to its source. Some later books and passages of the Old Testament exhibit what is called "the piety of the poor;" the poor are regarded as objects of God's particular loving care, and the rich have become synonymous with the oppressors. Even under the Israelite and the Judahite monarchies (in the prophets of the eighth and seventh centuries B.C.) it had become an assumption that no one was rich except by the accumulation of ill-gotten goods extorted from the needy. This may seem to furnish fodder for class warfare, as indeed it has and still does; one must and will discuss other sayings of Jesus (no more and no less questionable than the sayings about wealth and poverty) which suggest that whatever Jesus said, he never promoted warfare of any kind. It has long been a part of the conventional wisdom of the poor that anyone who is rich is either a thief or the heir of thieves. I think Jesus departed from this conventional wisdom.

Rabbinical wisdom exhibits a healthy indifference to wealth. The scribes were not wealthy and did not pursue a career which generated wealth. Like other wise men ancient and modern, they could be hired by the wealthy to serve their purposes. A claim might be made that what Jesus said about wealth and poverty could be derived from rabbinical wisdom; I do not know that this claim has ever been made. Rabbinical wisdom accepted from biblical wisdom the belief that wealth is the fruit of wisdom, meaning the intelligent and virtuous management of one's life and affairs. Wealth was God's reward and recognition of true wisdom. This is not the whole of biblical wisdom, but it is a large part of it; the book of Job is a dispute about the belief that poverty is the curse of fools, set forth with eloquence by Job's friends (and by Marx's source, the Reverend Mr. Townsend). We shall have to conclude that Jesus did more than echo the main themes of most biblical and rabbinical wisdom. More than a healthy indifference to wealth is expressed by saying, "You cannot serve God and Mammon."

I do not know that anyone has ever attempted to derive

the attitude of Jesus towards wealth and poverty from the Cynic school of Hellenistic philosophy, immortalized by Diogenes living in his tub. One may say that they sound alike, but the music is different. Diogenes was a professional eccentric, like the modern cultist who shows how independent and unconventional he or she is by rejecting socks and marriage. The "way" which claimed Jesus as its founder admitted no professional eccentrics, although it did not take them long to find their way in; Simeon Stylites was eccentric enough for any cult. I do not say the eccentrics were always wrong, and I shall have to deal with Francis of Assisi as an interpreter of the Gospels; but even he did not find a way in which everyone could be Christian. Francis needed Innocent III as Diogenes needed Alexander to practice his own eccentric way. Jesus needed no one, and he seems to have tried to communicate this independence to his disciples. There is nothing in the Gospels which suggests the wise man sitting scowling in his tub.

The frequent appearance of the Aramaic word *mamona* in rabbinical writings makes it possible that either Jesus or the scribes who preserved his sayings may have used an existing proverb to express his mind. It is probably because (in the popular and homiletic use of the Bible) the word "Mammon" has been personified as a rival deity that the New American Bible has replaced the word with the neutral "money." As a matter of fact that combination of the word with the word "serve," which in combination with the name of a deity usually means to worship, suggests that the personification of Mammon as a rival deity is not unfaithful to the thought of Jesus. It is not insignificant that the dictionaries give the meaning of the Aramaic word *mamona* as almost synonymous with the definition of wealth in one sense in *Webster's New Universal Una-*

bridged Dictionary quoted earlier: everything having economic value measurable in price; any useful material thing which can be bought, sold, or stocked. The word is also used in a non-neutral pejorative sense as it is used in Matthew and Luke, although my sources afford me no real parallel to the near personification of wealth as a rival deity. Whether the saying is an "authentic" saying of Jesus or an effort of the Gospel scribes to reconstruct or recreate his mind, it certainly sets up a direct contradiction to the ethos of western civilization about wealth as I have attempted to describe it. I would not be surprised if my summary were called a straw man.

But I do not think it is disputable that the saying is totally in harmony with all the other sayings attributed to Jesus concerning wealth and poverty. Before we pursue the discussion of these sayings, it is necessary to identify the "poor" and the "rich" of whom he spoke. We do not include slaves among the poor because Jesus and his contemporaries did not. No one then or now would claim that slaves were "better off" than the poor, whatever that phrase may mean; but domestic slaves were often better fed, clad and housed than the destitute but free poor. Throughout most of ancient history the sale of one's children, then of one's wife and finally of oneself into slavery was the last refuge from starvation. Figures for the percentage of slaves in New Testament times are hard to reach, and there is no doubt that they varied from place to place. The most recent estimate available to me is the guess that half the general population of the Roman Empire were slaves, running all the way from members of the personal staffs of the ruling classes to the lowest class of drudge (who gave the name to "servile work" in moral theology), the slaves who propelled the galleys and worked in the mines and in the baths, the athletic clubs of Roman gentlemen. Before the discovery of coal the warm baths were kept warm by constant stoking of the furnaces. Under Roman law the owner could not murder or physically abuse his slaves; this reaches a slightly higher level than Exodus 21:21, which says of the slave who dies the day after a beating that it is the owner's loss. But if the slave actually dies under the lash, the relatively humane law of Exodus 21:20 prescribes that the owner shall be punished; the law does not specify the punishment, but leaves it up to the judges (who were all slave-owners).

This digression was necessary to show that when Jesus spoke of the "poor" he was not speaking to or about a class which thought itself to be at the bottom of the social scale. If it is hard to get figures on slaves, it is equally hard to get educated guesses on the numbers of the poor and the rich and the degrees of poverty in which people lived. I wrote not long ago that Jesus probably never met a genuinely rich man in his life except Herod Antipas, and this meeting is attested only by Luke, not by Matthew and Mark. The rich who appear in the Gospel parables are the creatures of imagination. The famous remark of F. Scott Fitzgerald that the rich are different had more validity for the age of Augustus and Tiberius than it had for the 1920s when Fitzgerald wrote it. The wealthy did not live in backwater places like Palestine except on tours of government duty (which, in spite of Cicero's prosecution of Verres and the reforms of Augustus, was still a means of founding or enlarging a fortune). One can read about the wealthy of Rome in Roman writers (not much about the poor). One sees that they needed an army of slaves, which they had. One reads of Lucullus, who left his name to a gourmet style of dining (and, the last time I was in Beirut, to a sumptuous restaurant in that unhappy city). Lucullus did his tour of government service in Syria. One can read of Crassus (whose name survives in the adjective "crass" to designate tasteless display of wealth); he also did his government service in Syria and died there in a military disaster holding a post of command which he had no business holding. One can read of the nameless friend of Horace (I think it was) who fattened the lampreys bred in the pools of his estate by feeding them his slaves—a doubtfully credible anecdote. One can read of Poppaea, the wife of Nero, who demanded and got the milk of five hundred she-asses for her daily bath. And many others (those interested may read the satires of Juvenal); it is not my purpose to write a history of high life and conspicuous consumption in the Roman Empire, nor to verify Fitzgerald's saying for the times of Jesus. I do point out that Jesus and his fellow Galileans knew these rich only by hearsay. The rich have always generated hatred, but except for a few outbreaks (like that in France in 1793) it does not seem to have bothered them much.

Setting feelings aside, how many wealthy were there in the New Testament world? Again we are stuck with educated guesses. Including such fringe members of the wealthy class such as Zacheus, the tax collector, and Joseph of Arimathea, one of the Palestinian landowning aristocracy, it is estimated that the wealthy (meaning those who were not poor) were not more than five percent of the total population. There may be a similar figure for most of the modern world outside of those countries where western civilization is completely dominant. What the Roman world lacked (as the modern world outside of Europe and North America lacks) was a middle class. People who were neither rich nor slaves lived on the margin of destitution.

They lacked any cushion at all and were instant and total victims of any unforeseen disaster such as illness, injury or famine. The poor were profoundly grateful to the Romans for the *pax Romana,* the Roman peace which removed the normal scourge of war for more than two hundred years. They were also grateful for the most effective agencies of law and order which the world had ever seen, which for the first time (if not totally effectively) liberated most of the Roman world from bandits and pirates, who for centuries had looted the villages and raided them for slaves. The poor had no way of preparing for catastrophe, either personal or social; when it happened, they died like flies. Jesus' parable of the workers in the vineyard (Matthew 20: 1-34) is a good picture of casual labor in the Roman world (and in other times and places). Yet this dreary picture is not the point of the parable. Skilled artisans could look a little farther than the end of the current day when they thought of the future, although it seems that the rich had skilled artisans among their slaves; slave labor was for many centuries a constant threat to the free worker, whether skilled or unskilled. That slave labor at times became uneconomic (as it was becoming in the United States by 1860) is another story, and not an edifying one; but it does not appear in the background of the Gospels.

What Scott Fitzgerald said of the rich is equally true of the poor; they are different. These people, the vast majority of the population, were those whom Jesus is said to have addressed as blessed (Matthew 5:5; Luke 6:20). Both Matthew and Luke cannot preserve the authentic words of Jesus; "poor in spirit" (Matthew) and "poor" are not synonymous, although both designate the deprived 95 percent of the general population, as I hope to set forth shortly. Any translation fails to render the stark ironical paradox of the saying, which needs a genuine oratorical deliverance. Some imagination is necessary to see and hear Jesus, standing in a crowd (probably small—Jesus did not command audiences as large as the congregation which hears me on Sundays) and saying in a tone which I would not dare imitate, "Look at you, you hopeless, you lost, you doormats, you scum of the earth—you are the lucky ones! Do you believe that God loves you, that he is on your side, that he will take care of you?" Maybe Jesus could say that, and get away with it; I recognize that the paraphrase is utterly unworthy of the subject. I cannot get away with it, and I do not try—probably because I know that I do not really believe it. Jesus did not say, "Workers of the world, unite! You have nothing to lose but your chains." He did not promise them pie in the sky when they die. He said, "The reign of God is here, it is yours: I am telling you it is right on top of you, reach out and grab it." That is why the difference between "poor" and "poor in spirit" is insignificant in the context of Jesus's announcement of good news to those who never hear good news. "Poor in spirit" are those whose spirit is beaten down, trodden into dust by unending struggle and defeat and the contempt of their betters, deprived not only of wealth but of essential self-respect. It certainly did not and does not mean that ancient exegetical dodge which says that poverty of spirit is detachment in spirit from wealth actually retained.

Matthew arranges the beatitude of the poor with seven other beatitudes; Luke arranges it with three others and four woes, which are addressed to the rich, the well-fed, those who enjoy life and those who have a high social standing. It has sometimes been wondered whether Luke's more militant approach represents the authentic words of Jesus. I can say only that if they do not, they do not run counter to the general tone of unfriendliness to the rich which is undeniably present in all of the sayings attributed to Jesus. It is doubtful that Jesus ever delivered these eight beatitudes at one blow, as Matthew presents them. The beatitudes lump those who do not have the pleasures of the good life, those regarded as unimportant persons, the ill-fed ("hungry for righteousness" may be a refinement of the scribe), those who show kindness because they cannot afford to show anger, those whose purposes in life are uncomplicated by the pursuit of gain, those who reconcile because, again, they cannot afford to cherish grudges, and those who are badly treated because they do not let others dictate to them what is right and wrong. As a paraphrase, this probably does as well as others I have seen; and they seem precisely to praise those virtues which are more or less imposed upon the 95 percent by their social condition in a society more like ours than we like to admit. These virtues are, I say, more or less imposed upon them; Jesus had something to say about those who resist, and it is not a beatitude. To this I shall return.

What does Jesus mean when he tells the poor that the reign of God is theirs or in the parallel beatitudes, that they shall be rejoiced, that they shall be filled to satiety, that they shall see God and be called his children, that they shall experience the loving kindness which they do not experience in the present world? It takes very little knowledge of the religious background against which Jesus spoke (or in which his remarks were transmitted and no doubt transformed) to perceive that the language used in the passages cited is the language of eschatology. There is not much use in quarreling with the fact that for most of my contemporaries, whether in theological scholarship or out of it, this is the language of unreality. I shall have to give attention later to the question whether our common dismissal of eschatology may not be an evasion of a reality of supreme importance, admitting that the passages I have just quoted bears an uncomfortable resemblance to pie in the sky when you die. When I attempt to paraphrase the words of Jesus in terms which I hope my contemporaries will find more meaningful, I do not pretend to state things better or to imply that Jesus did not state them well. It is not a question of finding language within the reach of twelve-year-old minds. Our contemporary refusal to accept the language and the images of eschatology may imply a refusal to accept any reality which transcends human experience and scientific analysis.

If such paraphrases attempt to translate these words into promises which will be fulfilled only in some distant and unworldly future, I am not sure that unbelievers have not got something in their favor. This is no better than promises of a better future for posterity, or that a better world will be built after we are all dead, or that a time is coming when everyone will be a king or a queen, or everyone will be rich. Jesus spoke to real people with real needs and he promised them genuine relief right now. May I paraphrase him by saying that he promised them that complete fulfilment of their potentialities was within their personal reach right now and need not be put off until after their death? Let us say that he meant that the reign of God does not depend on wealth or other factors which are generally regarded as necessary for the good life; he meant that the good life is possible even for the deprived, the underprivileged, the powerless, the helpless. He meant, to anticipate what I shall try to set forth in the following pages, that wealth and other factors of that sort are obstacles to human fulfilment, to achieving or entering the reign of God.

He meant that you cannot buy or bully your way into the reign of God. I think most of us, when we have reached sufficient age and experience (more for some, less for others), have known and admired people who seemed to have achieved as complete fulfilment as anyone else without the accumulation of wealth or the pomp of social position. Yes, we do admit it; but, we say, if we were all like that, would it not play hell with progress and the collective achievement of the good life? Yes, it would; but would not this miserable world be a lot less like hell, even though it were less comfortable? This is rhetoric, and I should apologize for this appeal to sentiment; I risk it because it may be an appeal to honesty. Those who have never known or felt secret admiration (and even envy) for those whose life came closer to illustrating the beatitudes and seemed to lack nothing important may ignore this paragraph. If one were to go on to explore how these men and women found fulfilment and the really good life, one would have to go a great deal further than my present objective, which is to try to make some sense out of the attitude of Jesus towards wealth and poverty. I point out that there have been and are those who did make sense of his words.

Jesus spoke to the poor as one of them; when we stop to think about it, it is strange how little was remembered about his personal life, but nothing that was remembered suggested anything but poverty. He was identified as a carpenter (Mark 6:3) and a carpenter's son (Matthew 13:55); but these passages exhibit a patronizing tone in the speakers. The saying in which Jesus denies that he has a fixed home (Luke 9:58) does no more than place him in a large group whose numbers we do not know. In the Roman world, and particularly in Palestine, the numbers of the homeless were at least proportionately as large as they are in New York and Chicago, and it would not be rash to estimate that the proportion was much larger. It is not without interest that Jesus is said to have addressed numerous warnings against greed, avarice and conspicuous consumption to people who had very little wealth; this may suggest that actual poverty does not mean that one is free of greed, avarice and even of conspicuous consumption. Jesus, if the saying is authentic, seemed to look forward to no social millennium when poverty would be eliminated (Mark 14:1-6); certainly his sayings contain no hints of a social program for the elimination of poverty. Remarks attributed to him about the redistribution of wealth are addressed to the wealthy as individuals, and this we shall take up below.

It was to the poor of the first century that Jesus addressed the startling words recommending improvidence (Matthew 6:25-34; see Luke 12:22-31); at least, they would have to be so understood by any investment counselor who got passing grades at the Harvard Business School. If he were to tell his clients that God would provide for their needs—does he not take care of the birds?—they would soon find some other counselor. And indeed the words of Jesus are addressed only to the poor, those who lack the means to provide for the future, those whose needs are simple and elementary and satisfied by the frugal necessities. He does not say that God promises to provide us with an air-conditioned, split-level home or a high-rise condominium, with color TV in every room, with a freezer full of food and a pantry full of choice wines and liquors, with closets full of clothing from Brooks Brothers and Bloomingdale's, with a car or two cars and an RV and a swimming pool, with vacations in Miami or Las Vegas or

Hawaii, with college educations for the children. Do I exaggerate? Do I describe the expectations which our civilization makes realistic for the middle-class, and gives the poor the hope (at times illusory) that they can fulfil them when they rise to the status of the middle class? Such hopes and expectations can be maintained only by the kind of concern which Jesus repudiates. Life, he says—I paraphrase—is more important than this. Those who ask, "What is more important than this? This is life, this is sustaining life," can probably stop reading here, if they have not stopped earlier.

The saying about taking no thought for the future, a recommendation of pure unworldly improvidence, affords an excellent occasion for us to turn to the sayings attributed to Jesus which are concerned with wealth and are directed to the rich. In the world of the New Testament, as we have pointed out, the poor by definition could not provide for the future; this does not mean that they could not worry about it, but only the rich could exercise that concern of which Jesus spoke. We have already referred to what may be considered a key saying, the saying that the service of Mammon (wealth or anything which has a price) makes it impossible to serve God. The other sayings we shall consider take nothing away from the sweeping character of this saying.

But before we consider these sayings, we should advert to James 5:1-6 *(New American Bible):*

> As for you, you rich, weep and howl over your impending miseries. Your wealth has rotted, your fine wardrobe has grown moth-eaten, your gold and silver have corroded, and their corrosion shall be a testimony against you; it will devour your flesh like a fire. See

what you have stored up for yourselves against the last days. Here, crying aloud, are the wages you withheld from the farmhands who harvested your fields. The cries of the harvesters have reached the ears of the Lord of hosts. You have lived in wanton luxury on the earth; you fattened yourselves for the day of slaughter. You condemned, even killed, the just man; he does not resist you.

The sayings of Jesus about the rich, unsympathetic as they are, contain nothing like this ferocious invective. James echoes some of the Old Testament prophets (Amos 2:6-8; 6:3-7; Isaiah 3:14-15; 10:1-4; Micah 2:1-3). Jesus does not; and whatever we read in the Gospels should be read as the words of one who is said to have called sinners to repentance and to have excluded no one, even scribes and Pharisees, from his call.

We may first turn our attention to the saying addressed to the rich man whom Jesus invites to renounce his wealth and to become his disciple. The invitation is refused, and Jesus remarks that it is impossible for the rich to enter the reign of God (Mark 10:17-30; Matthew 19:16-30; Luke 18:18-30). The passage is as well attested as any of the sayings attributed to Jesus. It is found in both Mark and Q, and it is found without substantial variations in all three Gospels. It certainly meets the criteria set by Norman Perrin for an authentic saying: it owes nothing to biblical, rabbinical or Hellenistic wisdom, and it runs directly counter to all forms of conventional wisdom of the times known to us. It goes beyond the rebuke of the rich uttered by James, the Old Testament prophets and other sources. It presents a rich man who is under no reproach, who indeed is represented as a devout and observant Jew by all the standards of contemporary Judaism. Marks adds something said of no one else in the Synoptic Gospels, that Jesus loved him at this first meeting. The man must have had a good deal going for him; yet Jesus concludes the encounter with the regretful saying that he cannot enter the reign of God. The man is not a rich oppressor, nor is he a rich conspicuous consumer; he is just rich, and that does him in. That is not what Scott Fitzgerald meant when he said that the rich are different. It may have been what Jesus meant when he is reported (Luke 6:24) as saying, "Woe to you rich, for you have your consolation now."

It may help if we clear some exegetical rubbish out of the way before we undertake the discussion of the saying. I mention as a curiosity, but not as a serious problem, the theory that the "needle's eye" is an otherwise unknown name of a narrow Jerusalem gate through which a loaded camel could not be led. Perhaps I wrong the early interpreters. If the needle's eye were a narrow city gate, one got a camel through it by unloading the camel, which seems to be faithful to the mind of Jesus. The use of the word "perfect" (here and in Matthew 5:48) is more than an innocent distraction; I shall discuss this at once as an excuse of interpreters to convince themselves that Jesus could not possibly have meant what the saying clearly says. That this word is not "authentic" in the usual sense can be easily assumed and is generally accepted, but it makes no difference whether one thinks it is authentic or not. What Jesus is reported as clearly saying is that the rich man, just because of his wealth, cannot enter the reign of God.

Perhaps the most enduring and, I may say, the most pernicious interpretation of this saying is to make it an "evangelical counsel." This means that the rich man was invited to follow Jesus by electing a higher (Matthew, a "perfect") state of life. Poverty with chastity and obedience (given to a canonical superior) forms the basis of the "life of the counsels" or "the life of evangelical perfection" which in the Roman Catholic Church has for centuries been identified with the religious life, meaning a life lived in a community under an approved rule which specifies the ways in which these three counsels are to be sustained. It does not mean that the life of "seculars" (non-members of religious communities) is an irreligious or an imperfect life, although much of devotional literature leaves that impression. This state is entered and the obligations of the vows are undertaken by the free choice of the individual Catholic. No one is less a Christian and a Catholic for not undertaking the threefold vows; no one is told that by remaining a "secular" he or she cannot enter the reign of God. Jesus was not talking about this at all. The Catholic Church does not even exclude from the reign of God (assuming that it can do so) those whom it readily dispenses from the obligations of the religious life and the vows, although such separation often leaves a feeling of guilt, as I can attest. This is supported by such laws as those found in the old code of canon law (I have not consulted the new code on this) which exclude ex-religious from promotion to the ecclesiastical dignity of the monsignorate and from holding professorships in seminaries.

When I say that the theology of the evangelical counsels is pernicious, I do not refer to the works of the religious life, which for centuries has produced and still produces splendid examples of genuine Christian dedication. I refer to the implication that the Catholic Church fulfills this saying of Jesus because it has professional poor people whom it supports not very well, but somewhere this side (sometimes not very far) of beggary. This parade of the professional poor releases the "secular" members of the Church for the service of Mammon and concern for food, raiment and "the necessities" demanded for survival in the middle class of western civilization, as long as they share their Mammon and the fruits of their concern with the professional poor. It is something like hiring the lower classes to do the dirty work for the upper classes. It reminds me of the practice included in the act of military conscription of 1863 which allowed the man who did not wish to go to war to hire a substitute for three hundred dollars; a similar evasion was legal during the late Roman Empire. It is no wonder that some of the American poor (mostly Roman Catholic immigrants) rioted quite violently in reaction. The parallel between religious and hired substitute soldiers is not perfect, but it may deserve some thought. The existence of religious does seem to have given Catholics the same feeling of comfort and security which citizens have from the possession of an army, such as the citizens of the United States had from the possession of the United States Cavalry in 1880. It is of interest that the number of religious has declined sharply within the last twenty years.

There is no biblical law and no ethical system which forbids the acquisition and accumulation of wealth; and if Jesus said that the rich man could not enter the reign of God because of his wealth, he certainly denied the freedom of choice which is presupposed in the theology of the counsels. The man is not free to follow Jesus and retain his wealth. I think the authenticity of the saying is supported by the response of the disciples, which is twofold. First, "Who can be saved?" They caught his meaning. Secondly, "Look at us—we have done it, and what do we get?" The answer to this complacency is found in the whole of the Gospels; a quick answer was given by Jerome in a homily

on the passage: "What did you give up?" Jesus is not
reported to have dealt with these responses by the theology
of the evangelical counsels or by other evasions; he said,
"You are right—it is impossible; but what human beings
cannot do, God makes possible." The answer to the boast
of the disciples must be an allusion to the abundance made
possible by a sharing of wealth—not abundance by the
standards of opulence; as I said above, Jesus never promised that to anyone. He promised enough as I said above,
for all. And this brings us to the radical reality of the Gospels, the reality of grace; but this is too large a question for
me to take up within the limits of my chosen topic. There is
just no calculating what grace can do. I understand that I
am not touching the most important truth of the Gospels.
Perhaps it is too much for me. I do know that the cult of
Mammon leaves no room for grace; if you have enough
Mammon, who needs grace?

If we reflect on what it may be that makes it impossible
for the rich man to enter the reign of God or to be a disciple of Jesus, we ask questions which Jesus did not answer
but which he compels us to ask; and when we seek the
answers we may be wrong, a possibility which the writing
of this manuscript keeps me constantly aware of. I ask the
reader, if he or she finds that I have given the wrong
answer to these questions, not to deny that they are genuine questions. I have referred to Francis of Assisi, who
found an answer to his questions about wealth and poverty
which many have admired and almost no one has imitated.
I believe that if Francis had been less of a blithe spirit and
more of the kind of organizer that Ignatius Loyola was or
a popular orator with the qualities of Bernardine of Siena,
the authorities of church and state would have united
against him as they did against Girolamo Savonarola, who

has never been proposed for canonization, and would have treated Francis the same way. They did so act against the Franciscan Spirituals of the fourteenth century, who were neither blithe spirits nor organizers nor popular orators. Francis organized nothing and was not dangerous. Neither did Jesus, but even the most devoted admirers of Francis would not deny that Jesus had something which Francis lacked. The admirable and venerable Order of Friars Minor (in its several varieties) is not the creation of Francis of Assisi nor does it follow his way of life.

Francis found the answer to his questions, and it was not altogether different from the answers found by Christians as early as the third century; he renounced wealth by withdrawing from the world, on which he depended only for what he could beg. Francis, like the monks of the desert, depended on Catholics who had not renounced what he had renounced but had acquired enough wealth to share some of it with him. Jesus never proclaimed withdrawal from the world of humanity as a way to the reign of God, nor did he in his life, as we have any record of it, illustrate such a withdrawal. What I am going to suggest is that the Catholic Church may have failed in its mission by not becoming Franciscan; if it had become poor like Francis, several of its leaders might have died like Savonarola. The Italian noble families who ran both church and state in the Italian peninsula in the fourteenth and fifteenth centuries took their money very seriously.

Most exegetes have taken it as a myth, probably of Lucan construction, that the primitive Christian community of Jerusalem practiced community of goods, by which all the believers pitched their wealth, great or small, into a common pool from which all were sustained. The major reason for this skepticism is the absence of any reference to such a practice in the writings of Paul, not only in his own churches but even in his references to Jerusalem. And he does refer to that church when he urges the members of his churches in Greece and Asia to contribute to the great need into which the Jerusalem church had fallen, probably in the famine in the reign of Claudius. Paul did not present a plea for Christian communism, but he did write some lines (2 Corinthians 8-9) which every Catholic fund-raiser should be compelled to memorize. He says simply that the superfluity of some should compensate for the privation of others so that "a certain equality" may be reached. Yet we can be sure that this letter was written to a community which was almost entirely poor; Paul tells us as much. I am not much impressed by some recent efforts to make the church of Corinth middle-class. How could the poor have superfluous goods? Anyone who has ever been poor knows that there are degrees of poverty. One must have recourse to the tired old adage that when anyone is in need, anyone who is not has superfluous goods.

Both Luke and Paul were trying to find some way in which Christians and the church could live with this and other sayings of Jesus. The solution of Luke was not found practical even in New Testament times (with a possibly un-just assumption that first century Christians were more likely to accept poverty than we are). I think, however, that Luke may have grasped the mind of Jesus better here than most of the modern interpreters of Jesus. It occurs to me that our colleagues might apply to their interpretation of these sayings what Vincent Taylor said about the saying on divorce (Mark 10:2-12). There is no doubt, Taylor com-mented, that Jesus said this, and there is no doubt about what he meant; with all due reverence, we must abandon him. I praise the candor and honesty of the late Dr.

Taylor; I recommend both to the serious consideration of my colleagues. Paul was ignorant of economics and social engineering; but if there were those in dire need who were not helped he knew the reason why help was refused, and it was not the complexity of the problem.

It is no mystery why Christians have refused to take Jesus at his word, and refused to admit that one cannot be his disciple if one retains one's wealth. The Christian community, if it is genuinely Christian, renounces wealth and the pursuit of wealth, either for the individual members or for the community. While Paul shows no knowledge of the Christian communism of goods which Luke portrays at Jerusalem, he does believe that the saying of Jesus that wealth should be given to the poor should be minimally fulfilled by seeing that no one is in dire need; he says expressly that their generosity should accord with their means and not go beyond them, and that they should not impoverish themselves to relieve others (2 Corinthians 8:12-13). This last recommendation puts him socially behind some contemporary theologians.

But does even Paul, who must still be regarded as a fairly good interpreter of the mind of Jesus, exploit the sayings of Jesus to their fullest? Let me suggest that this might mean that the followers of Jesus should form a community in which wealth is individually renounced, in which wealth is neither pursued nor accumulated, in which there were no destitute and any superfluity which might accrue because of the frugality of the standard of living of the members would be dispensed to the nearest needy. Does this sound like the community of New Harmony (in early nineteenth century southwestern Indiana) which failed? Perhaps we ought to allow Christianity as many practical failures as we have allowed the pursuit of wealth, individual and social.

The Christian community would differ from attempted communist communities by the simple fact that the Christian community would act entirely by the free consent of its members with no coercion. Such a Christian community would deal with the problem of wealth the way the Mennonites and the Brethren and the Friends deal with war; it just would not have any. Frankly, I do not see how a community or an individual person can claim the name of Christian without some such renunciation. As I said earlier, it would play hell with progress; maybe it is about time someone played a little hell with progress, another name for Mammon. Do I feel assured that I am right about this? No way; I am groping, I do not know that I have caught the mind of Jesus. All I am certain of is that the church in the modern world of western civilization does nothing about this problem.

Did not Jesus have rich friends? Jesus withheld his friendship from no one; he was criticized because he seemed to like low company. When one tries to enumerate these rich friends, one runs into a little trouble. The mysterious Simon the leper who was the host to Jesus and a party of guests seems to have been a man of means (Mark 14:3-9; Matthew 26:6-13; Luke 7:36-50); he was not so surely a friend of Jesus. Joseph of Arimathea, who buried the body of Jesus, was certainly a man of means and he is said to be a disciple (John says he was a secret disciple because of fear: Mark 15:43-46; Matthew 27:57-60; Luke 27:50-54; John 19:38-42). Martha and Mary and Lazarus of Bethany can hardly be called rich because they gave Jesus a dinner; they were not rich enough to have domestic slaves, which meant that they were not rich. The tax-farmer Zacheus (probably the local agent of the absentee magnate who had the contract) is not really described as a friend of Jesus, and he was an agent of a wealthy man rather than a wealthy man himself. He claims that he gave half his goods to the poor (far more than I give, if you must know), and nothing suggests that he began this only when he met Jesus. The point can be made that if Jesus had rich friends and rich disciples, he did not greet them at this first encounter with what he said to the rich young man (Matthew made him a "young man" and the title has stuck). Of course, we do not know how many of them said what the rich man said to him: "What else should I do? What is wrong with me?" Sooner or later the disciple must ask himself that question, and it need not be about wealth. It is a legitimate question whether the "rich friends" of Jesus remained rich if they became disciples.

There is a collection of anti-rich parables—it seems that they must be called that—peculiar to the Gospel of Luke. Exegetes have long noticed and discussed an anti-rich bias in the third Gospel, and in recent times they have discussed how faithful this bias is to the "authentic" words of Jesus. Certitude is not within reach on this question, but it is not essential to the search for the mind of Jesus. I described this mind above as unsympathetic towards the rich, and the degree to which a lack of sympathy is thought to veer towards unfairness depends on the sympathy with which the viewer antecedently beholds the person under discussion. I suppose there are those who would think that a lack of sympathy for child molesters would be excessively harsh or lacking in compassion. If Luke displays in his tone a harshness towards the wealthy which one believes did not exist in the "authentic" words of Jesus, one will have to deal with a clear lack of sympathy in some passages of the other Gospels. Jesus was sympathetic towards the rich with the sympathy which he exhibited towards Pharisees, tax farmers and prostitutes; they were sick and needed the physician. Like many of the sick, they did not recognize their illness and refused the cure. Such a refusal was recorded to have been once called by Jesus the sin against the Holy Spirit (Mark 3:29; Matthew 12:32; Luke 12:10).

The collection of peculiarly Lucan parables is found mostly in Luke 10-19, "the journey narrative." In fact the rich appear as the principal characters in most of these parables, but wealth is not always the point; the parable of the Samaritan (10:25-37) presents a rich man who is the very model of the love of one's neighbor. This is hardly an illustration of an "anti-rich" bias. Luke does not exhibit a doctrinaire hostility towards the rich; being rich, like being a scribe or a Pharisee, is not an inescapable destiny of spiritual ruin.

The parable of the rich fool (Luke 12:16-21) is close enough to doctrinaire hostility towards the rich perhaps to satisfy those who think that Jesus was not sufficiently unfriendly towards them. The rich man is not represented as an oppressor of the poor (except by definition) nor as lacking in compassion, but only as enjoying the security his wealth gives him; and for this he is a fool. The only threat which he has and of which he seems unaware is the threat of imminent death, for which no one can plan. He also faces the dissipation of his wealth at death. He seems to have no heirs nor to have made the provision which the laws allowed; but as a rule one should not press the parables too closely in details. The point is not who will get the man's wealth, but that he will lose it. I really do not know how much this parable goes beyond the bit of New England folk wisdom contained in the anecdote about the Yankee who, when asked how much money Old Man X left at his death, responded with Yankee terseness, "All of it." It says the same thing in the form of a story which the saying about care and worry says, which immediately follows the parable in Luke (Luke 12:22-31) and the saying about corruptible treasure (12:32-34; see Matthew 6:19-20). The parable says it with more sharpness and the application of the epithet "fool" to one who shows such care and prudence and takes so much pleasure in amassing savings.

The parable about Dives and Lazarus has become a classic description of the unfeeling possessor of great wealth in the immediate presence of destitution (Luke 16:19-24). The perils of making this parable the single key to the mind of Jesus on wealth and poverty are discussed in an appendix to this chapter. The reader of the parable should note but need not believe (as I do) the opinion of many interpreters that the dialogue between Abraham and the rich man (16:24-31) is a primitive expansion of the original parable. This does not affect the clear meaning of the story of Dives and Lazarus. The misery of Lazarus is no concern of Dives; he did not cause it, he cannot change it (we may assume that Lazarus is just one out of many), and as far as he can see he is not obliged to do anything about it. The modern reader may find a touch of unrealism in Lazarus lying practically in the doorway of the rich man's dining room, and the picture is a bit unrealistic; but the doors of a genuinely wealthy man were a place of assembly for all sorts of petitioners for his bounty (Latin *clientes*), and in fact the Roman wealthy made arrangements to scatter some bits of bounty for these petitioners; *noblesse oblige* and all that. As I observed, we should not press the parables in details. No one has ever found the picture of the rich man who feels no compassion for the destitute exaggerated. It may even speak to those who are not rich but who are also not destitute. The parable sends this man to hell literally for not doing anything.

What should he have done? Would it have been another parable if Dives had let Lazarus scavenge the leftovers from his dinner? I do not know; Jesus told his parable (I rather believe he told this one) and I am entitled to tell my own, but not to rewrite his. What Jesus said to Dives is what he said to the rich young man: get rid of your wealth to Lazarus and his kind if you want to enter the reign of God. No, giving Lazarus the leftovers (which Lazarus would have found too rich for his tastes) or even inviting Lazarus to join him might not have been enough. Jesus, however, in another parable did praise one who invited all the hungry of the neighborhood to join him at dinner; parables are parables. Certainly I cannot imagine Jesus telling a parable in which Dives would have referred Lazarus to the nearest dispensary of food or food stamps; somehow I have the feeling that he would still have been buried in hell. He would still have done nothing. It is not just for being a conspicuous consumer that Dives is damned, although this is not counted in his favor. The question rises (whether one asks it or not) if it is possible either in the Roman world or in the contemporary world (or in any world which lies somewhere between) to be a conspicuous consumer without being a bastard like Dives? I will no longer listen to any one who claims that the middle class contains no conspicuous consumers. In the world of redefinition into which we have passed we need a redefinition of conspicuous consumption.

Parables, like myths, create a world of their own and follow a logic of their own. It is a world created by imagination which is quite fictitious and quite unreal; etymologically parables are synonymous with myths (the Greek *mythos* is a story). To be convincing the parable must reflect the world of experience; by the art of the story-teller this world is sufficiently distorted to emphasize the point which the story-teller wishes to emphasize with a clarity which reality rarely has, and only for the perceptive. The parable does not teach; to the imperceptive and the unreflective it says nothing, as reality says nothing. It raises questions; when skillfully told it compels us to ask questions, although no amount of skill can give light to the blind who refuse to see—who say, "What has that got to do with us?" To quote Horace again, *de te fabula narratur;* it is about you that the parable is told. The questions which the parable raises can be answered only by the reader or the hearer of the parable; in a sense the parable says something different to each one, because each one frames the question and the answer which arise from the parable.

I wrote the following composition for an oral presentation to a small audience some years ago. When I wrote it I had the beginnings of some ideas about this book in mind. The composition was never published, and it seemed to say well enough what I want to say in concluding this chapter that I reproduce it with no more than the necessary scrubbing and polishing. I wanted to say that the sayings of Jesus about wealth and poverty are addressed to the poor as well as to the rich; when I found this among my papers, it appeared that I had already said it.

APPENDIX: A WORD FOR DIVES

One of the most effective sermons I ever heard was a practice sermon I heard delivered in a seminary nearly fifty years ago. The speaker, a fellow student (since deceased), paraphrased and expanded the parable of Dives and Lazarus and concluded his discourse rather abruptly with the Gospel sentence, "And the rich man died and was buried in hell." The rather difficult audience, which was a seminary community at dinner, was not often left in stunned silence. I now wonder, either from worldliness or from cynicism, whether the preacher was not a bit unfair to Dives.

Dives has long been the stock example of a man who went to hell for doing nothing. Have we been so anxious to send Dives to hell that we are trying to send Lazarus to heaven for doing nothing? This is reward without either works or faith. When it is put in those terms it does not seem quite fair. So it should not be put in these terms. Jesus did not so put it, if we are to read the parable as expressing something like his mind, and we interpreters are accustomed to warn ourselves against allegorizing the parables. The parable is a short story, and conclusions from the parable are drawn by us, not by Jesus. Many interpreters think that the dialogue between Dives and Abraham is such a conclusion, added to the parable even before the parable reached Luke. The story describes a man so unfeeling that his enjoyment of his pleasures is undiminished by the sight and presence of pain which he can relieve. The scene is unreal, but we allow that in fiction. The lack of compassion which is described is not unreal. The added conclusion punishes Dives for having and rewards Lazarus for not having; and at this point I feel that someone should put in a word for Dives. After all the parables do raise questions rather than answer them.

It is beyond dispute that the Gospel sayings of Jesus exhibit a clear bias against wealth and the wealthy and in favor of poverty and the poor, the class to which Jesus himself belonged. There are no Christian directions for the acquisition and the use of wealth. The Gospel sayings, I believe, do not express the clear and rather crass statement made by revolutionaries that the rich are by definition thieves. A study of the social and economic world of the New Testament might, I am told, support the statement for that period. The same study indicates a valid estimate that 95 percent of the population lived in grinding poverty on the margin of destitution. Jesus said nothing in favor of this economic system. Is it allegorizing to identify Dives with the five percent and Lazarus with the 95 percent? I think it is, but we can let that question hang in the air. Lazarus suggests Job, the very paradigm of suffering in the Hebrew Bible. I suppose Jesus could see this as well as I do. Job is also the paradigm of the innocent sufferer. He has been deprived of everything because God wishes to win a bet with Satan. When one allegorizes Lazarus as the innocent sufferer, one may get into trouble.

If Lazarus reminds one of Job, Dives reminds one of Job before his fall in his wealth and sumptuous living. Job was not, like Dives, without compassion. He asserts in his own defense that the hungry were never turned away from his door. He also complains that such generosity did not protect him from falling into destitution. If Lazarus, the impoverished Job, had encountered the wealthy Job instead of Dives, we would have a different parable. The parable of Jesus did not deny the possibility of a wealthy Job; that would be an impossible distortion of reality.

Since we are in the realm of fiction, let us suppose that Lazarus encounters another Lazarus. In this hypothesis he may get sympathy, but he will get no help. If Dives in a fit of generosity were to spill a crust on the floor, would my parable become unrealistic if I were to represent Lazarus A and Lazarus B fighting for it rather than sharing it? But even if they did not fight over a single crust, Lazarus and his peers can give each other nothing but compassion. If Lazarus travels on the road from Jerusalem to Jericho, he will be safe from bandits. If he should fall into their hands, they will probably be members of his peer group. It is unlikely that they will beat him because he has nothing, but it has been known to happen. If they should, the Samaritan who picks him up had better be as well fixed as Dives. Another Lazarus may not do any more for him than the priest and the Levite.

I have remarked that the impoverishment of Job has no explanation in terms of human experience. Neither does his wealth; it is a given without which there is no story. Similarly the destitution of Lazarus and the wealth of Dives are not explained, nor need they be; there are rich and there are poor. Without them there is no story; we do not find them unreasonable presuppositions, as we find the presuppositions of the tragedy of Oedipus. But when we encounter such things in real life, we ask questions; real life is concerned with persons, not with types. We ask of a real Lazarus what happened to him; we know he is not a test case for a bet between God and the Devil. We ask of a real Dives how he became so unfeeling.

Let us first deal with Lazarus. Let us stipulate that he does not fall under the generality uttered by the author of 2 Thessalonians 3:10 (somewhat illiberal in modern social thought): if any will not work, let him not eat. Since Jesus told fictitious stories for expository purposes, let me tell or rather recall a story which I did not compose. It is one of the stories of Sinbad the Sailor in the *Arabian Nights Entertainment*. Sinbad was walking along the seashore when he came upon a crippled and helpless old man who asked for his assistance. Sinbad gave him his arm to lean upon, but soon that was not enough. Before long Sinbad was carrying the old man on his shoulders. The old man had a grip of iron, and he grew heavier as the journey proceeded. Finally Sinbad realized that the old man would kill him; so he killed the old man.

Like the stories of Jesus, this story includes no moralizing and no discourse. It carries implications and raises questions, which each reader must perceive for himself or herself. I shall not moralize, but I shall ask one question. If Lazarus turned out to be the old man of the sea, would we have a different parable? If so, then I have another generality under which Lazarus should not fall. Perhaps the story of the Good Samaritan gives me still another. Lazarus and his friends are not to deal with Dives or with the Good Samaritan as the thieves dealt with the traveler on the road to Jericho. I can at least raise the questions and find my own answer. I will say that anyone who sees the bandits of the Jericho road as social reformers is not talking about Jesus or his words at all.

So when we ask questions about a real Lazarus, we find, without leaving the world of parables, some categories which make him, shall we say, a less urgent object of our compassion than some other people. He should not be one of the non-workers of Thessalonica; he should not be a bandit; and he should not be an old man of the sea. The parable matches the ideal needy person with the ideal uncompassionate person. The imaginary encounter may clarify our understanding of real life, but it is not real life.

I said one must ask of the real Dives how he became so unfeeling. There is no single explanation of a real Dives; there are many ways in which compassion is stifled, so many that it seems easy. I read of a prominent and respected woman who spends about $1,000 a day on her person. I realize that published gossip is not always truthful; I do not expect the lady to publish the accurate figures on her expenditures. I thought of the celebrated Roman lady, Poppaea, the wife of Nero, and wondered how much milk of she-asses would be provided by this sum of money. Apparently most people feel this needs no explanation, so why should I? It is none of my business. I suppose I mention it because I would not want it to be thought that my modest word for Dives extends to sympathy for that sort of thing.

So let me suggest that Dives may feel no compassion because he has identified Lazarus with the non-workers or the bandits or the old man of the sea. He is wrong in making this identification, but he is not unreasonable if he asks to be shown his error. If he has become insensible to the needs of others, if he is really convinced that their need is always deserved, then perhaps not much can be done for him. He has turned Lazarus into a type and abdicated all responsibility for him. In this he may be returning the compliment the friends of Lazarus have paid him. In dealing with a real Dives as in dealing with a real Lazarus we run the risk of imputing motives. The author of fiction can create motives for his characters. When we do this for real people it is still fiction.

I would like to return to a question I raised earlier. I said that Lazarus cannot expect any real help if he encounters another Lazarus. Whatever we think of Dives, only Dives can do something for Lazarus. Dives is equipped to do good which Lazarus, no matter how big his heart is, can only dream about doing. If Dives should be seized by a fit of generosity, Lazarus may be embarrassed to find a way to return his generosity.

I would like to return also to my observation that in the

parable the wealth of Dives and the destitution of Lazarus are both givens with no explanation of how they came to be what they are. In real life these questions are asked and they can be answered. In real life one does not answer these questions by having recourse to typical figures—by saying, for example, that Dives is an oppressor and Lazarus is a deadbeat. The real Dives has done things and had experiences which enable him to assist the destitute rather than to be destitute, and other experiences which have made him unwilling to assist the destitute. The real Lazarus will have a different history of deeds and experiences which have deprived him. No doubt some moral deviousness is possible in the analysis of each case, but that certainly takes us beyond the parable. And I do not think that Jesus implies a moral evaluation which would demand that Dives become Lazarus so that Lazarus can become Dives. Each must save his soul in his own way, and that would be another parable.

I was once asked by some students what I thought the prevailing modern religion is. Without much thought and more to stimulate discussion rather than to arrest it, I answered, "Demonology." For a hasty answer it was better than I thought. All of us, believers or not, explain our problems—we do not solve them—by blaming demons. In the contemporary context Dives is a very useful demon. He does all wrong and leaves every one else innocent and feeling noble. In a world where Dives is exorcised and nobody but Lazarus and his peers are to be found the reign of God has come—hasn't it?

TEMPTATION II: IN THE OLIVE GROVE

IT IS night in the spring in the valley of the Kidron, just east of the walls of Jerusalem. The narrow valley threads between the steep slopes of the city and the mountain of the Temple, crowned by the bristling walls of Herod's new buildings, and the more gently rising but much higher slopes of the Mount of Olives to the east. Late in the evening hours the people of Jerusalem and the surrounding villages have retired for the night, and the full moon of Passover is near the zenith. In the bottom of the valley is a small grove of olive trees. Where the brightness of the moon is shaded by the branches of the trees Yeshu sits upon the ground. He is alone, but dimly visible some yards away and out of the range of hearing of a normal speaking voice there are three sleeping figures; they are his companions. Yeshu shows evident signs of an intense mental struggle; he almost resembles a victorious boxer, stunned and marked from the conflict but master of himself. He sits silent and brooding. Suddenly through the trees strides a figure, jaunty and self-assured. He approaches Yeshu and is greeted by him.

YESHU: So it's you again. I might have expected you. At a time like this the last thing I need is a visit from you.

NICK: Your plans have not gone well, have they, Yeshu? Your friend and disciple will be here shortly with the police, and when you see how these, your chosen followers behave, you will know that you have nobody.

YESHU: That was a low blow even for you, Nick; but I was surprised he went so cheaply.

NICK: So was I, Yeshu; the poor fool did not know how much it meant to me to trap you right where you live, in the middle of your chosen ones. I would have gone much higher.

YESHU: Gloating should be beneath you, Nick.

NICK: It isn't gloating, Yeshu; somebody had to show you that you cannot win against me. There is no one I cannot buy to do my work. Do you think I came here just to gloat? I came because I am sure you have learned that you need me, but I don't need you.

YESHU: Then why don't you just go to hell, if you will pardon the expression? I don't need you.

NICK: I suppose Adonai is going to send you a dozen legions of angels? Yeshu, Adonai and I have been around each other a long time, and I can

tell you for sure he does not work that way. I
do not need even one legion; all I need is one
cohort of stout, well-trained Roman legionaries, and I have them right up there in the An-
tonia. Haven't you learned that I own the
Roman establishment? A word from me in the
right places, and those legionaries will be here
so fast that those shabby Temple police will not
even know what hit them. Yeshu, this is my ter-
ritory; do not say you do not need me. You
never needed me so much in your life.

YESHU: Are you offering me another deal?

NICK: Deal! Listen, Yeshu, beggars cannot be choos-
ers, as I think you have pointed out more than
once. I am offering you your life, a chance to
go back to Nazareth and the carpenter shop,
get married and have children, and die in a
peaceful old age, and give up this silly proclamation of the reign of Adonai. I do not know
what you are up to, but I do not like it. You
have a choice between that and getting crucified tomorrow. Have you ever seen anyone crucified, Yeshu? I think you have. Let me tell you
it is not fun and it is not funny. Yeshu, I like
you, in spite of the fact that you have treated
me quite rudely. I had some good ideas for
you, and you could have served me well. But
you do not really believe in me, and I will not
lean on you. Just accept the gift of life which I
am offering you.

YESHU: Nick, I know you mean well, but you are smart enough to know that I cannot and will not put myself in your debt. There is something I have to do and I have to do it tomorrow, and neither you nor anyone else can stop it or change it. I cannot explain it to you—you would not understand; everything you stand for is opposed to what I have to do. Believe me, if I did not know that this is what Adonai wants, I would never do it; I would make any deal you want.

NICK: Be crucified? Adonai wants this? You must be out of your mind. He never said anything like that to me. What do you think this is going to accomplish?

YESHU: Start the reign of Adonai, which means the end of you, Nick. I see torches up on the hill; I think they are coming. Will you be at the show tomorrow?

NICK: I would not miss it for the world. It will be a pleasure to get you out of my hair.

IV. SALVATION THROUGH POWER

You said in your heart; I will scale the heavens;
Above the stars of God I will set up my throne.

—Isaiah 14:13.

I HAVE tried to argue that Jesus was remembered as saying nothing about the acquisition and the management of wealth. It seems to follow that there is in no proper sense a Christian way to be rich, either for an individual or for a group. I must now turn to what I take as the second pillar on which western civilization reposes; like wealth, it is assumed, it is taken for granted, it is above criticism. This assumption can be seen in the very designation of *civilization* which we are accustomed to give our culture and our way of life, the term which we oppose to other cultures which we designate pejoratively as *barbarian, savage* or *primitive.* It is not my intention to resuscitate the myth of the noble savage, or to propose that primitive mankind is mankind before the fall—although Rousseau had more going for him than he realized. My observation is that Man is and has always been a bastard, but that his worst features are emphasized and supported by western civilization. When the Pilgrims encountered for the first time the rigors of a Massachusetts winter, they were helped to survive by friendly Native Americans. In only a few years the campaign of two hundred and fifty years to exterminate the friendly Native Americans had begun.

Civilization is derived from the Latin word *civis* which we translate *citizen,* a member of a political community (not merely a dweller; slaves, women, children and foreigners were dwellers). The designation *political* is derived from the Greek word *polis* usually translated "city-state," which the Greeks thought was the only truly human way of life in a community. People who did not live in *poleis* (that is, the rest of the world) were dismissed by the Greeks as *barbaroi,* people who did not speak Greek but babbled a kind of subhuman noise. The term included such peoples as the Egyptians and the Mesopotamians, who had invented arithmetic and monumental architecture before the Greeks had come down from the trees. Snobbery is one of the oldest and best established traits of civilization.

When we say *civilized* we imply politics, a political way of life in society. It seems worth noticing that the Greeks, from whom we have the word *politics* and the earliest expression of political ideals and political theory, showed almost total incompetence in managing the affairs of their city-states, which proved to be a political form incapable of maintaining itself for more than a short time. Politics is the civilized way of organizing men and women in large numbers for a common purpose, and of mobilizing the human resources of the community to obtain objectives which lie beyond the capacity of a kinship group, however large such a group may become. This is accomplished through the kind of authority which is called political, distinguished from the older and simpler kind of authority found in kinship groups, called domestic or familial or paternal (by a word which has recently become obscene, patriarchal). Domestic authority cannot go beyond the extended family, which can be quite large; political authority reaches all the citizens, even those not related by kinship or not even known to each other personally. The scope of political authority is and has long been a topic of dispute (and quite often of armed warfare), so we may say that it has never been established just how wide and deep its scope is. It seems safe to say that it is as wide and as deep as those who hold authority can make it. Political authority has always been despotism tempered by the rebellion of the subjects.

Politics means a distinction between persons who bear authority—the "government"—and others who are ruled by authority—the "governed." This distinction exists in all forms of government. It is somewhat blurred by certain myths attached to the idea of democracy. One of these myths was perhaps never better stated than by Abraham Lincoln when he coined the phrase "government of the people, by the people and for the people." Those who use this much quoted phrase seem to forget that Lincoln did not describe a political reality but a political ideal, and that he urged his listeners to take up the unfinished task so nobly advanced by the honored dead, to see that government of the people, by the people, for the people should not perish from the earth. I think he knew that no government, including the one over which he presided, had ever been anything but government of all the people by a few of the people for the same few of the people; and I think he knew that it would remain that type of government for a long time to come—as we know, until the present moment.

But even modern democracy makes only a hollow pretense to be anything but a government of the few for a few; before the nineteenth century politics did not pretend to be anything else but what the Greeks called oligarchy, government by the few for a few. Governments are what they have always been, devices by which some—whether more or less is really irrelevant—can impose their will upon others and feel morally good while doing it. I say the numbers are irrelevant because a tyranny of the majority is no less a tyranny because it enjoys wide popular support. On the other hand, the Athenian *demos* of the time of Pericles, the mother and head of all democracies, numbered 14,000 adult males in a population of 100,000; this illustrates well the distinction between the government and the governed, even in the original democracy. If one counts the life of the Athenian democracy from the death of Pisistratus (527 B.C.) to the battle of Chaeronea (338 B.C.) one gets a total of 189 years, an age which the United States has barely reached since the Constitution was ratified. As governments go, the Athenian democracy endured better than any version of the French Republic since the Revolution.

When we look at the distinction between the government and the governed, we may see in it a perpetual obstacle to the unity of the political community. As it so often happens, the Greeks had a word for this; the word was *stasis*. *Stasis* (it is almost impossible to translate this word) meant the splitting of the political community into factions which had different and opposing objectives and were unwilling to compromise either on the objectives or on the means to reach them. Each faction identified its objectives with the "public good" and regarded opposing factions as enemies of the public good—that is, of the state. They were not dissenters, they were traitors. Ancient Greek theorists saw *stasis* as the chronic illness of the Greek city-states which regularly became so acute that the state could be saved from self-destruction only by the forceful imposition of one-man rule, which the Greeks called *tyranny*. The word was not as pejorative in Greek as it is in English. But it did mean that the tyrant had to suppress some of the much prized Greek *eleutheria*—freedom. But even ancient Greek sources describe the Athenian tyrant Pisistratus as a good thing for Athens, except that an Athenian who had lost even some of his freedom thought himself not much better off than a barbarian. In any case, the *stasis* of the Greek city-states was responsible for their collapse before Philip II of Macedon, who should not be reckoned among the benefactors of humanity. He ended permanently in Greece both *stasis* and *eleutheria*.

What the ancient Greeks described as a disease of the body politic does not seem to be the same thing as a strife of political parties for power in modern democracies, at least the one in which I live. I emphasize that it does not *appear* to be *stasis;* it could become that. Of other countries of which I have no inner political experience I must say as an outsider that it often looks like *stasis* to me. Perhaps the citizens would say that it is not when seen from the inside, as I say about politics here. If an ancient Athenian were asked to review our American situation, he might ask to be shown where the difference lies. I would tell him that no member of either major party wants to destroy the political system which has given his party power in the past, gives him a share of it in the present and may be expected to return it to a majority position in the future. Power is the name of the game, I would explain, not who happens to hold it at the moment. As you Greeks buried *stasis* when you fought the Persians and did not bury it when you tried to fight Philip of Macedon, so our Democrats and Republicans will unite and fight like heroes against anyone who tries to destroy the system which has been so good to both parties. And that, my Athenian friend, is why our democracy (blessing myself while I utter the word) will last longer than yours—until someone like Philip of Macedon appears who is willing to raise the market price of politicians. After all, it was not just by the superior power of the Macedonian phalanx that Philip subjugated the Greek city-states.

A dispute over who is to govern is politically meaningless until the dispute is raised by those who are, have long been, are traditionally accepted and accept themselves as the governed. In politics the way for the governed to escape their place has long been to join the governing class. When the governed are refused this opportunity and their numbers are large enough, the potential for a revolution is present. But governments have been astute enough to know that in the history of civilization revolutions are rare, and successful revolutions are even rarer. Good politics has always included a recognition of reality, reality being how much you can yield and still retain power. Government, which means politics, means that there will always be a ruling class and a ruled class; because politics is the art by which some (more or less) impose their will upon others.

We come, then, to the question of the common good or the public good and the governing or the ruling class. The Latin words *res publica,* from which "republic" comes, means "the public good." Historically the public good has been what the governing class said it was; this is not the same as saying that the public good is the good of the governing class, but I may hazard the suspicion that the governed class has usually found it hard to tell the difference. In spite of the myths of democracy and popular sovereignty, the governed class still finds it hard to tell the difference. The slave-owning author of the Declaration of Independence coined the immortal statement, "just governments derive their powers from the consent of the governed." For him the governed did not include slaves any more than it included livestock (although a gentleman planter of Virginia would have found it obscene to breed with his livestock, but not with his slaves). He meant the consent of some of the governed. For Mr. Jefferson the "sovereign people" not only excluded women but also those adult males whom he and other members of the land-owning gentry thought too irresponsible to be trusted with the franchise. Irresponsible meant impecunious. Mr. Jefferson lost his battle to the landless. As a classical scholar he probably knew that the Roman Empire enjoyed the consent of the governed for hundreds of years. His republic has not yet survived as long.

The governing class has long thought and still thinks that it can trust no one but itself to make prudent decisions concerning the public good. This confidence is based on the pool of intelligence, education and experience which can be found among the members of the ruling class in contrast to the much smaller pool which can be found in the ruled class. The governing class is well aware that it contains as many fools as the law of averages allows; it believes it can be trusted to prevent these fools from reaching positions of more than minimal responsibility. It does not trust the governed to police themselves as carefully; and it is only fair to say that this confidence has long been justified in spite of occasional failures. I hold no brief for the ruling classes in our democracy; but I know nothing that would make me hold a brief for their replacement by the ruled classes. I may quote Lord Acton, tiresome as it may be: no matter who you are, power tends to corrupt. It comes to this: the ruling class, like the wealthy class, is indestructible. Perhaps this is because they usually coincide. But Hammurabi of Babylon (1728 B.C.) inscribed in his code of laws that the gods had appointed him to succor the weak and the oppressed. I have no reason to think that he said this any more or any less hypocritically than the contemporary politician in a modern democracy says the same thing. Hammurabi was an absolute ruler at the head of an oligarchy, the governing class of his day. I am still waiting for the politician who will convince me that he does not represent the governing class of our day.

How does the governing class get the governed class to do its will? That is to say, what is the basis of its authority? It may be cynical to say that the basis of political authority is physical force, the power of coercion. It is true that sound political theory will maintain that the basis of political authority is moral, what Jefferson as cited above called the consent of the governed. This does not free democratic governments from the necessity of maintaining an army and a police force, from severely regulating even the private possession of weapons which can be used against persons and from prohibiting the organization of private armies. The efforts of the United States units of government to suppress the private armies of organized crime have often been ridiculous; but the laws are there, they have often been reduced to practice more successfully in other countries and would be here if politicians did not so often verify their claim to be the world's second oldest profession. Earlier pre-democratic societies were more candid about the ways in which authority had to be maintained; a rough estimate of the number of modern democratic governments which would survive the night if the use of physical force were at one stroke abolished leaves one wondering about power derived from the consent of the governed. I am probably as "good" a citizen as you can find in the sense of observing the laws and fulfilling my civic duties; but I would stop paying taxes at once were it not for the gentle threat of coercion, as most of my fellow citizens would, and for reasons which do not obviously betray unmixed self-interest.

Does it really make much difference how our vaunted law and order prevail in our public affairs, or whether discipline is secured the way the captain of a pirate ship secured it from his quarterdeck? Yet in fairness to pirate captains it must be said that no pirate ever retained his authority over his crew without the consent of the governed. Individual malcontents, like rejected captains, walked the plank or were hanged from the yardarm. I think Jefferson would have recognized pirate captains as genuine Jeffersonian Democrats, as long as they limited their depredations to Spaniards and other Papists; indeed, he would have recognized pirate captains as responsible citizens who had enough money to be trusted with the franchise.

No, it does not really make much difference how law and order are secured. When governments think they are in desperate straits (whether they are or not) from their own citizens or subjects, they defend their authority the way Blackbeard defended his. We should not confuse the exercise of political authority with the ownership and use of slaves. I have dealt with slaves under the topic of wealth, because that is the heading under which slave-owning societies have dealt with them. Again, the difference may not always have been clear to the slaves and the lowest members of the governed class. To them it was the imposition by force (let us for the moment drop the hypocrisy about "moral") of the will of another, and that was all there was to it. The wise slave owner, like the wise manager of free labor, tried to keep workers so busy and so fatigued that they had little time to brood about rights and duties.

We have, of course, emerged from the thousands of years during which slaves were a commodity. One hesitates to say that any human institution which endured for at least six thousand years did not have something going for it. From the point of view of the ruling class it certainly did; and by definition the slaves had no point of view. We must look at what has often been called (quite inexactly) the modern form of slavery in most of western society, and that is the wage contract. I am not looking at it from a social or economic point of view, or even from a moral point of view; experts have studied these aspects of the question far more fully than I, and they are qualified to do it, as I am not. But it is an aspect of the human condition which as a Christian, a theologian and a human being I cannot pretend is unimportant to me or to the literary enterprise in which I am engaged, and I cannot wait for the experts to tell me what opinion I should form. For the wage contract is a vital cog in that vast complex machine which we call western civilization. I treat it under the heading of politics rather than under the heading of wealth because it seems to come under the manipulation of people rather than the manipulation of wealth, and because capital and labor for over a hundred years have both employed politics to achieve their ends in the area of wages.

I have only two observations to make about this, neither of which seems to have much merit; surely this is modest enough. The topic will come up again when I turn to the sayings attributed to Jesus which seem to be pertinent. The first observation is that the wage contract must be one of the major causes of civil dissension and strife in the modern industrial world. During most of my life observers have said that if genuine civil war ever breaks out in the United States, it will erupt between the working classes and employers and those who sympathize with either side. Apart from any theological consideration, the question of wages has brought the modern industrial nations as close to the *stasis* which destroyed the political life of the ancient Greek city-states as anything else. It is, I believe, no longer merely a question of wealth (if any question of wealth can be called *mere*). It has become a question of power, and not the same sort of dispute as exists between Democrats and Republicans. The two political parties need each other to survive; but class warfare tends to the mutual destruction of the contending classes. I know this objective is impossible, but do you expect me to discuss class warfare as if it were something reasonable?

The second observation is that the wage contract historically has been the most recent and the most civilized way in which the governing class gets the governed to accept the imposition of the will of the governors. The threat of dire need or starvation or, in recent times, of descent to a lower standard of living, has been sufficient to make the governed sit up on their hind legs and beg with only rare recourse to cruder forms of persuasion; the Pinkertons are an extinct species. My random reading took me a few years ago to a popular book on the Molly Maguires of Pennsylvania in the 1870s. I know that the contemporary managers of business and capital do not employ the tactics of the anthracite mine operators of nineteenth century Pennsylvania. It remains true that the operators violated no law and that throughout the twenty years of bloody strife in the mining counties they were supported by the full panoply of law, the courts and the armed force of the Pennsylvania police, assisted by the operators' private army of police. It is also true that the Mollies struck down none of the magnates, who lived in Philadelphia, New York and London, but bushwhacked nearly two hundred members of their own working class. It is impossible to be sympathetic either with the Mollies or with the mine operators, both of whom carried organized inhumanity to new heights.

But one knows that the operators could have done something to change the situation; they had the power, and the ball was in their court (the play on words is, I assure you, spontaneous). One cannot compare the Mollies, who represented the working class at its lowest level (from which it has not entirely emerged), with the modern industrial worker who strikes to retain his color TV and his recreational vehicle and his paid vacation. The Mollies, God rest their souls, had not made it to the middle class. They did not even commit crimes, which they did, because the floors of their shacks were bare earth instead of wood. They committed crimes because their human dignity had been trampled; one can praise neither the response nor the treatment to which the response was given. There must be some way in which men and women can be paid for their work without going through what the industrial world has gone through, but you must not ask me how; I am not an economist, and like the economists I have no answers. Jesus may have had a few things to say to this point; but apparently he had neither the wit nor the education nor the sophisticated understanding of modern social and economic realities to say anything worth the attention of any sensible person who lives in modern industrial society.

I believe I have dwelt at length sufficient for my purpose on politics as the institutionalization of the will of some human beings imposed upon others. I have yet to consider it as the means of imposing the will of some social groups, whether they be tribes or the various varieties of civil society, upon other groups. The social organization which makes possible the progress which we call civilization exhibits throughout its history an optimum size beyond which the human race has not yet found it possible to go. The largest as well as the most enduring political society which has yet arisen on the human scene is the Roman

Empire. I have remarked before that the Roman Empire achieved political successes which have never been equalled; I must add a remark based purely on personal taste, made in an earlier writing, that it is impossible to study the ancient Romans closely and remain sympathetic to them. The Romans achieved the reality of the "sovereign state," which in modern international politics has become a buzzword. The nation-state has become a sovereign agent of disunity, and feeble efforts to approach this problem such as the defunct League of Nations and the moribund United Nations are just that, feeble efforts. They were planned failures, dishonest in their conception and in their execution. They mask but do not take away the reality of the quarreling sovereign nations, each dedicated to its self-interest and its right to assert itself. The patriotic duty of each statesman is to defend that self-interest and that self-assertion; to fail to do that minimum would be treason.

Whether such wounds to the human community as ethnic hostility and racism are born of the nation-state or are supported by it is probably beyond answer and may be regarded as idle philosophizing. What is plain beyond dispute is that such problems are insoluble as long as the sovereign nation-state dominates international politics. Some members of some contemporary minorities sometimes seem to speak as if they were the first people to suffer oppression because of ethnic or racial difference. I am compelled to remark that both are nearly as old as humanity and that oppression is wider and deeper than ethnic and racial prejudice. Whites enslaved whites thousands of years before they enslaved Blacks. The rationalizations employed in ancient times are rarely available; we know that Aristotle, the master of them that know, was convinced that some people are naturally slaves. That may be the grand-daddy of all ethnic and racial rationalizations. The roots of Christian anti-Judaism (and of Jewish anti-Christianism) are deep and tangled and beyond my powers to discuss here. That would need another book, and I doubt whether I could expect to live long enough to write it, or that it would do more than offend both Jews and Christians. That is probably enough reason not to write it, although both deserve to be offended. I believe some of the sayings attributed to Jesus have a bearing on this problem, probably not direct enough or too well balanced to satisfy those who feel most deeply concerned. For my present purpose it is enough to point out that these wounds in the fabric of the human community will have no healing in any kind of external or internal politics yet devised by humanity. Do you think they will be healed by passing laws or constitutional amendments, or by having enough wars or armed combats until the contenders are all killed off? Let those who think so say it; I shall continue to wonder who is unrealistic or unworldly.

We come, then, to the normal means used in international politics by one country to impose its will upon other countries. The first and the normal means is diplomacy; the regard in which this skill is held is attested by the commonplace that a diplomat is one who is sent abroad to lie for his country. I have read enough newspapers in the last seventy years to know that it is not true, as another commonplace has it, that truth is the first casualty in war; in diplomacy truth was never alive to be a casualty. Diplomacy must be understood in a large sense, so large that I cannot and should not attempt to define it; let me try to illustrate my meaning by a few examples.

As a literate citizen all I know is that the United States imposes its will on all the Americas south of its border with

a few sporadic exceptions; I suppose I would offend
Castro by calling him sporadic (25 years is sporadic?) The
United States has achieved this with a minimum use of
force over a long time. The Romans, the most successful
peace keepers who ever ruled, maintained thirty-five
legions on their frontiers. A legion at full strength (most of
them were not) was a force of 10,000 men. The United
States has not achieved this diplomatic *tour de force* merely through conversations held by men in frock coats and
striped pants sitting around mahogany tables. What the
United States has used instead of force is not a matter of
public record; if it were, I would have less nasty suspicions,
remembering what we did to the Cherokees and the Sioux
and the assorted tribes who were sent on the Trail of Tears
by that great Populist Andrew Jackson. Maybe, like the
Romans, it is impossible to study the people of the United
States closely and remain sympathetic to them. I doubt
whether I go beyond evidence or reasonable conjecture if I
sum up the diplomacy of my nation as the manipulation of
other nations to one's own purposes by a judicious combination of lies, promises insincere or not kept, bribery
and threats. Red Cloud, the great Sioux chieftain, said that
the white men had kept only one of all the promises they
made to him; they said they would take his land, and they
did. When diplomacy as I have described it fails, nations
turn to what Clausewitz called the extension of politics. I
quote this because every one else does, not because I ever
read it in context.

The extension of politics was earlier called—I believe by
some medieval writer whose name escapes me—the *ultima
ratio regum,* the final argument of kings. The two phrases
effectively say the same thing, which I may roughly
paraphrase in popular language: if I cannot persuade you

to do things my way, I will knock your block off. The finest skills of educated intelligence and the sciences in the most advanced and sophisticated civilization have not advanced international disputes beyond the level of the street brawl and are themselves dedicated to be the best brawler, which means to kill so many of the adversaries that they must give up. Between nations as between persons the block is ruled by the biggest and the strongest bully. Why is there no police force to put these bullies in their place? Mostly because no nation wants to yield the possibility that it might be the biggest bully. An international police force, or even an international consensus repudiating bullies as moral lepers, can be established only at the price of the national sovereignty which we hold so dear. Nations still resolve their disputes by the code of the duel, but with less honor; the duel was controlled violence, and those who were not gentlemen were not permitted to engage in duels. Commoners are not only permitted to engage in wars, they are drafted for military service by the gentlemen. And wars settle nothing except the question raised by Humpty-Dumpty: the question is who is to be master, that is all. Maybe that is the only valid political question.

Those of us who are old enough can still remember the stench of self-righteousness with which the victors in the Second World War tried to perfume themselves to cover their moral decay. I say this to meet those who respond to my belief in the moral bankruptcy of war with the feeble plea that at least in that war the issues between good and evil were clearly matched. To accept the fact that National Socialism was morally intolerable does not mean that I must embrace the rotting moral corpses of the "democracies." These demonstrated the justice of their cause by the bombings of Dresden, Hamburg, Tokyo and Hiro-

shima, by assisting at the subjugation of a dozen countries
and hundreds of millions of people to a tyranny which our
own leaders now call the worst known in history, and by
thus creating the balance of terror in which we now uneasi-
ly survive. Millions of people died to bring this about? Are
these the political leaders and is this the political thinking
and planning from which we are to expect the creation of a
new and more beautiful world? I have never thought politicians could establish much of a claim on my loyalty by
assuring me that they are not Nazis; but when you think of
it, that is all that most politicians for the last fifty years had
to say for themselves.

The final argument of kings is well illustrated by a
sculpture from pre-dynastic Egypt (which means earlier
than 2800 B.C.). This work is known as the palette of
Narmer; it is a decorated platter in which cosmetics were
mixed. One side represents the victorious Narmer standing
over a defeated enemy chieftain seated on the ground. In
one hand he grasps the hair of the enemy; in the other hand
he brandishes an enormous mace with which he is about to
bash in the enemy's skull. Narmer meant it when he said,
"You do it my way or I'll knock your block off." He is the
first statesman in history to be portrayed doing his thing,
vindicating his state's sovereignty and honor and probably
its right to natural resources. I am surprised that a copy of
the palette of Narmer is not hung in foreign offices all over
the world; it ought to be, at least in the foreign offices of
those nations who think they can play Narmer (with never
a thought that they might have to play the other role). The
Assyrians decorated the walls of palaces where they received foreign (usually subject) ambassadors with relief
sculptures representing Assyrian victories and their treatment of the vanquished, often impaled on stakes. The

Assyrians were political realists, and they wanted their visitors to share their realism. Finally the subjects did; not a tear was shed when the Assyrian Empire was wiped out in war, a thing which they had done so well, in 608 B.C.

For some years I have been presenting to my audiences—or to anyone who is willing to listen—my exposition of the theory of the morally just fornication, or the morally just adultery, or the morally just rape, or the morally just child-abuse. This usually comes over as a clumsy or clever (depending on how sympathetic the listeners are to what I am driving at) effort of wit, rhetoric or sheer absurdity, or as downright offensive. I have never tried to tell listeners how deadly serious I am, and I will not try now. Just let my effort speak for itself. Like war, all the activities just mentioned imply certain effects for quite innocent people who happen to be too close to the action. These unpleasant effects can be tolerated as long as certain good (or morally indifferent) effects are intended as the purpose of the action; and I have drawn up a kind of moral yardstick which renders an easy and quick judgment possible. After all, in most of these activities there is not much time for deliberation.

Let us take the apparently most difficult case, the morally justifiable rape (in most modern ethics the other three are a piece of cake). First there must be a sufficient cause. Such a sufficient cause exists in a compulsive and irresistible desire for satisfaction, whether sexual or sadistic or vindictive. This desire cannot be suppressed without the risk of serious harm to the psyche of the person who desires it, and may do great harm to others if satisfaction is not given promptly. Secondly, there must be a due proportion between the good to be achieved and the damage which must regrettably be inflicted on one person. This proportion exists because the good of the psyche of the rapist is of a higher order than the mere physical good of the victim. She (usually) may suffer some psychic damage, but that is obviously not intended and is not the object of the rape, so it is not a means to an end and is an evil which may be tolerated by the principle of the double effect. Furthermore, the victim has it in her (his) power to neutralize any psychic damage by simply accepting the pleasure. Thirdly, there must be no damage done to innocent parties. One may not rape others besides the one intended nor do any damage besides that required to consummate the rape; for instance, one may damage a resisting victim or a bystander who attempts to assist her (him), but only with due proportion between the damage done and the end to be achieved. Fourthly, rape should be employed as a last resort when all other means to achieve satisfaction have been tried and have failed. This is verified if the rapist has been totally unsuccessful in his efforts to seduce or purchase women (men or boys). Fifthly, there must be a reasonable hope of success. For a healthy and vigorous adult who seeks his victim in solitude this should furnish no problem. Measure your own reaction to this proposal; if you do not like it, you will know how I feel about the ethic of the just war.

If I have greatly over-simplified this, all I can say is that it is about time someone did. I know what is wrong with my ethical theory; raping people is wrong. So also, according to a popular song, killing people is wrong. There is something fallacious about the thinking which finds illicit sexual relations intrinsically evil, but killing people morally neutral; all you need is a sufficiently good reason. Why that does not work for sexual intercourse I do not know; I am just too old to split moral hairs in this kind of stunt. There has never been a morally justifiable war; to find one is like discussing the number of angels who can sit or dance on the point of a needle, and about as useful in discussing how one may live a Christian life.

For my assistance in over-simplifying let me invoke Mark Twain, the genial agnostic who was one of the most humane gentlemen to appear on the American scene. He wrote for posthumous publication a short story called *The War Prayer.*[1] In this work he so successfully skewered the hypocrisy of Christians that I must quote at least the prayer, which he says expresses the unspoken desires of those who pray for victory in war. I doubt that Mark Twain ever heard of the moral principle of the double effect; but with his own matchless literary skill he held it up to the ridicule it deserves.

> O Lord our Father, our young patriots, idols of our hearts, go forth to battle—be Thou near them! With them, in spirit, we also go forth from the sweet peace of our beloved firesides to smite the foe! Lord our God, help us to tear their soldiers to bloody shreds with our shells; help us to cover their smiling fields with the pale forms of their patriot dead; help us to drown the thunder of the guns with the shrieks of their wounded, writhing in pain; help us to lay waste their humble homes with a hurricane of fire; help us to wring the hearts of their unoffending widows with unavailing grief; help us to turn them out roofless with their little children to wander unfriended the wastes of their desolated land in rags and hunger and thirst, sports of the sun flames of summer and the icy winds of winter, broken in spirit, worn with travail, imploring Thee for the refuge of the grave and denied it—for our sakes who adore Thee, Lord, blast their hopes, blight their lives, protract their bitter pilgrimage, make heavy their steps, water their way with their tears, stain the white snow

with the blood of their wounded feet! We ask, it, in the
spirit of Love, of Him Who is the Source of Love, and
Who is the ever-faithful refuge and friend of all that are
sore beset and seek His aid with humble and contrite
hearts. AMEN.

Oh, Sam Clemens, we needed your voice when your
great-hearted fellow Americans dropped bombs on Hiro-
shima and Nagasaki which vaporized a couple of hundred
thousand civilian non-combatants, bleating about the lives
of American "boys" which were thereby saved. But you
were dead, and it seems no one of us had inherited your
humanity or your literary skills.

To my surprise, I have lived long enough to read a statement published in 1984 by the Roman Catholic bishops of
the United States which really questions the legitimacy of
war as an extension of politics. Some have found the statement too strong and some have found it too weak; considering the sources of the criticisms, the statement must be
so balanced as to be just about the right statement for this
time and place. That a stronger statement will be made I
have no doubt; I have tried to make a stronger statement
here, but I do not speak with the weight of the bishops nor
with their responsibility. I said earlier that I remain a Catholic because it is the only game in town. It is very reassur-
ing to learn that the game is still being played. It is rare that
leaders step out in front instead of waiting to see which
way the parade is going.

One of the oldest poems in the western world is written
on the theme of war, which the author (or authors) whom
we know as Homer called "man-ennobling war." Homer
knew quite well that this is what war is not; the nobility of
his characters emerges in spite of the horror of war, not be-

cause of it. When Priam begs for the body of his son Hector from his killer, Achilles fails to the same non-heroic state as the petitioner and shows himself both more and less than a killer. The poets have paid tribute to war, but I know no truly great poet who liked it. That was left to lesser men; Tyrtaeus and John Lovelace are as well known as they deserve to be. John Courtney Murray was one of the greatest men of my generation (and that is one of the few things I will fight to say). He was a just-war-ethics man; even a man of his magnitude had his blind spot. But in a wiser moment he said it is difficult to discuss something as basically irrational and immoral as war.

I find it so easy to write with sarcasm about war that I feel almost like a patronizing physician discussing the troubles of a mentally defective child. People do not really like war; they hate it and they hate what it makes them do and what it does to them. But they say they have to do it. That is what the compulsive rapist says. One wants to say, then why do you not stop it, give it up; but it is like trying to talk reason to a drunken sot. People need a new perspective on life and on what is important and valuable. That new perspective our western civilization has lamentably failed to give those who must live in it. It is time to turn our attention to what Jesus may have said about this perspective, and to ask ourselves whether we really want peace if peace means giving up the fruits of war. Or perhaps we would rather wait until the fruits of war turn to Dead Sea fruit.

As I read over what I have written, I realize that I might as well throw it away (which I am not going to do). I have heard my friends talk about politics and I have disputed with them, and I know quite well what I sound like on the topic. I sound cynical; I make politics the object of a display of cheap wit; I trivialize important, even vital public issues. I show the same indolence and despair which made it possible for Hitler to rise to power in Germany and ultimately in most of Europe. I have heard all this, I know what it means, and I am aware that by publishing things like this I will hear more of it. I do care when my friends are disturbed because of me and even find me offensive. It is impossible for me to share their faith in the political process and to believe that anything will be accomplished through politics to change or even to improve temporarily the wretched human condition. I have no faith in politics simply because I have dabbled in history. I judge politics by its record, which is now 5000 years old. Politics has never produced the good life for any but a chosen few in any generation, and that has been produced only by the infliction of misery upon many. It is no different in the contemporary generation. There is still blood on every commodity we use. I was reminded of it again this morning when I took my breakfast of orange juice, cereal, a banana and coffee. Every one of those damn items got to my table at the cost some human misery, not my own.

Am I proposing a kind of Christian anarchy? I am proposing nothing; but when I reflect upon politics and the heroes it presents to us for our choice in the election year in which this is written, I wonder whether Christian anarchy may not have more in its favor than has yet been brought forth. The attitudes and the habits and the skills and the ethics which go into the prosecution of a successful war are the same attitudes, habits, skills and ethics which go into the prosecution of any successful political effort. They can be summed up in one phrase: kill the bastards. They are all illustrated in the relief sculpture of that early politician

Narmer, which says, "You do it my way or I'll knock your block off." I appreciate the faith in the political process exhibited by so many of my friends; I cannot share it because it is faith in the morally justifiable rape.

V. SALVATION THROUGH WEAKNESS

How the oppressor has reached his end!
How the turmoil is stilled!

—Isaiah 14:4

WHEN we take up the sayings attributed to Jesus which touch upon politics, we find that they are extremely few; and the problem of finding his "exact words" (or the pseudo-problem) is as vexing here as anywhere. There is no difficulty in finding in the sayings of Jesus a sufficient number of allusions to wealth and poverty to permit us to establish certain attitudes about wealth and poverty; and we can say with some confidence that if we do not know his actual thinking on wealth and poverty, we do not have and cannot discover his mind on any topic. This would compel us to say that on the basic problems of human existence he said nothing, and that these problems must be met (and solved if possible) with no reference to his words or to the fact that he existed. I wish I were sure that Christian theologians do not shrink from this conclusion.

No such assurance is to be found in his thinking about politics. The sayings which touch on this problem are so few that we can and will discuss them at some length. But it is necessary before we take up the sayings to establish briefly (and as well as we can) that Jesus did not live in a politically inactive community. If Jesus himself was uninterested in politics, as the sayings in the Gospels (or the absence of them) suggest, his neighbors were not; and while I never draw parallels between him and myself, I think that he must have encountered questions like those I have encountered: "What do you think of Senator McCarthy?"

[Joe, that is]—"What do you think of Senator McGovern?"—"What do you think of what we are doing in Viet Nam, or the Near East, or about disarmament?" If Jesus answered such questions as the Gospels suggest he did, with "I don't know" or "I don't think" or "Who's he?", I suspect his answers would have been found as negative and irresponsible as mine have usually been.

All we know from ancient sources contemporary with the life of Jesus indicated that the area in which his entire life was spent was not much less politically active than the same area has been for the last forty years. No doubt many villagers were passive spectators, but the modern Palestinian villager may be as good an indicator of the political vitality of the villager in the time of Jesus as some monograph written for a dissertation here or abroad. Anyone who thinks that the contemporary Palestinian villager is politically moribund has either never been in a village or never taken the trouble to talk to anyone who has. About 30 years after the death of Jesus the Jews of Palestine rose in insurrection against the Roman government. It took the Romans, who were rather good at this sort of thing, about seven years to put the insurrection down. This kind of movement is not mounted by a handful of activists who throw up barricades. The one question which Jesus could not have avoided except by withdrawal from society was: "What do you think of the Romans?" The Gospels tell of one occasion on which the question was asked.

Perhaps the first observation to be made about the sayings of Jesus concerning politics is that he said almost nothing. If we assume that the atmosphere in which he lived was charged with political intensity which he felt like others, then the Gospels have filtered out almost all of what he said. This is simply not tenable. The Gospel sayings preserve many utterances which deal with human behavior in the trivial and commonplace situations of ordinary life. Surely in any hypothetical sayings not preserved about contemporary politics there must have lurked some wisdom which even the sources of the Gospels would have esteemed as exhibiting more enduring values. At least one such saying was preserved. I have concluded—and I am fully aware that the conclusion is disputable—that Jesus regarded political wisdom and counsel as just as valuable and just as important as wisdom and counsel on the acquisition and administration of wealth or the prudent disposition of investments.

The Jewish historian Josephus, a contemporary of the apostolic church (regarded by his contemporaries as a renegade) wrote of four "philosophies" among Palestinian Jews of his time. In grouping the four "parties" or "sects" he may have been counting apples and oranges. In any case, the four were the Pharisees, the Sadducees, the Essenes and the Zealots. They were not four different and varying political parties. With reference to the major political question of the day, the Jewish response to Rome (let me over-simplify), the Sadducees embraced Rome, the Pharisees split, the Essenes withdrew but finally joined the Zealots, and the Zealots were irreconcilably and actively anti-Rome. In the terms of Josephus, Jesus can be placed in none of these groups. This is somewhat remarkable. The Gospels and their sources may be presumed to have shared the political prejudices of their time, as all people, including my friends and I, do. They do not describe Jesus even in these terms. The simplest explanation of a non-political Jesus is that Jesus was non-political, and that the reality of Jesus resisted the most obvious transformation, one which every historical character experiences at the hands of his biographers. It takes more than the skill of some putative redactors to account for this.

The fact remains that Jesus was executed by the Romans for the crime of rebellion. The fact also remains that the proceedings of the trial of Jesus were reported by no one who was present in a form which has survived; the Gospels attest unanimously that the disciples escaped arrest by flight. We do not even know the terms of the charge nor the quality of the evidence; and while the Romans did not follow the procedures of British and American common law, the founders of European jurisprudence did show some interest in evidence. The execution of Roman justice was remarkably prompt, but so was the execution of justice in Great Britain, Canada and the United States into the twentieth century. In spite of the almost total lack of information about the trial of Jesus, Christians and others have always believed that the trial of Jesus was a gross miscarriage of justice, however it was brought about. This belief has not been overturned by some recent efforts to show that Jesus was really a Zealot.

Since it is obviously impossible to identify Jesus with the Pharisees or the Sadducees without scrapping the Gospels entirely as sources of information about his life, there is no place left to place him in contemporary politics except with the Zealots; the Essenes in 30 A.D. seem to have opted out of politics. While placing Jesus with the Zealots also seems to demand scrapping the Gospels, this has seemed to some interpreters preferable to a Jesus who had no interest in politics. I am not sure that *The Passover Plot* of Hugh Schonfield (which I reviewed unsympathetically) deserves mention as a serious book, in spite of the fact that it sold 250,000 copies. Mickey Spillane, the creator of Mike Hammer, sold at least twice as many and the historical scholarship of the two authors is roughly about the same.

But the late S. C. F. Brandon took his work more seriously and presented all the evidence available to show that Jesus was at least sympathetic to the Zealots; that is to say, the execution of Jesus was not a total miscarriage of justice. Brandon did not convince his colleagues that the case for Jesus the Zealot could be supported, and hence I do not think I am obliged to do any more than accept this scholarly consensus. The Zealots were what in modern times are called freedom fighters; modern freedom fighters of the same type explode bombs in hotel lobbies, but the Zealots did not yet have bombs. The Romans called them bandits and nicknamed them *sicarii* ("knife-men"), after their tactic of stabbing their targets in crowded streets. One of Brandon's ideas (I am not sure that it was original with him) was that *Iscariotes,* Iscariot, was a Grecized form of an Aramaic effort to pronounce this Latin word, and that "Simon the Canaanite" was a mistranslation of Simon the Zealot. Without saying anything about the linguistics, this argument appears to me as convincing as an argument would be that because of the calling of Matthew, Jesus was a tax-collector or that because of the calling of Peter, Andrew, James and John, Jesus was a fisherman.

The Romans, like most governments, did not distinguish sharply between freedom fighters and bandits. Perhaps it was their failure to make this distinction which made the Romans the last government in the area of the ancient Roman province of Syria (and you can throw in the ancient Roman province of Asia) to suppress banditry in those areas. If Jesus can be trusted to have said anything at all, he renounced violence; and interpreters have preferred to think that his words are irrelevant to politics, which should be discussed without any reference to anything he said, did or was. I shall raise a question or two about this.

The first saying I shall discuss is attributed to Jesus when he was arrested. It is found only in Matthew (26:52) when Jesus refuses any attempt at armed defense: "They that take the sword shall perish by the sword." My purely subjective opinion is that this saying has a savor of standard popular wisdom. In similar wise sayings interpreters are not afraid to assume that Jesus was quoting traditional wisdom rather than adding to it. The context does make it unlikely that Jesus chose that moment of confusion and disturbance to drop a quotation from popular wisdom; here Mark and Luke present a more credible picture. All the Gospels agree that Jesus refused armed defense, whether he quoted this *bon mot* or not.

Did he refuse it because it was hopeless? Like the authors of the Gospels, I was not there. But Jesus and his companions were not threatened by a detachment of legionaries, but by a crowd (Greek *ochlos*), size not mentioned. The cohort mentioned by John (18:3) cannot have been present, as the other Gospels knew. If they had been, they would not have delivered Jesus to the priests. John, written at least two generations after the events, assumed that Roman law and order would not have permitted the operations of a private police force. We know that in the Temple area they did. There was no reason why, in the judgment of Peter and probably of others, a quick determined resistance might not have effected the immediate objective, escape into the darkness. Peter's swordsmanship was about as good as his theology, but certainly the servant of the high priest (probably in charge of the operation) was rendered *hors de combat* for a moment; others were startled and frightened, and a moment was all that was needed. The fact remains that at the only time in the life of

Jesus, as far as we know, when the use of arms might have been to his advantage, he refused it. Whether he said what Matthew quoted is really irrelevant. It is a nice quotation, and sums up the futility of weapons in a nutshell. But we do not need it to establish that Jesus was totally opposed to the use of violence for any purpose, and therefore I have seen no necessity to argue this uncontested truth. Whether politics is possible without violence (war, said Clausewitz, is an extension of politics) I shall leave to others to argue; all I know is that politics without violence has been impossible. I set aside discussion of Gandhi, a unique case. I wrote some years ago that Jesus taught us how to die, not how to kill. I think that still stands.

The next saying I shall discuss is the only saying of Jesus which at first glance appears to be concerned with politics, the most clearly (meaning with the fewest variations) attested saying in all three Synoptic Gospels, and most likely of all the sayings of Jesus to be "authentic." This is the saying about tribute to Caesar (Mark 12:13-17; Matthew 22:15-22; Luke 20:20-26). The saying was certainly "Give Caesar what is his and give God what is his"; the framework of the question to which this saying is an answer is not so certainly original. I think it is original because, as I have said above, this is one form of the question which Jesus could not have avoided. The question was, "Is it 'right' to pay a tax to Caesar?" The word "tax" represents one and the same word in Mark and Matthew (a Grecized Latin word), another and a proper Greek word in Luke. One need not look for an exact vocabulary of tax revenue either in the evangelists or their sources; the one odious word "tax" is clear and sufficient. The word "right" attempts to render a somewhat ambiguous Greek word; in the context it must refer to moral liceity as it often does.

The questioners are not asking about general moral principles; if one were to add the phrase "for us" to the question it would not falsify its meaning. The questioners were not interested in whether it was right for Alexandrians or Antiochenes or Ephesians to pay taxes to Caesar, nor by what right Caesar demanded taxes. He exacted taxes by right of conquest; and since it was hardly 100 years since Jewish kings had exacted taxes by the same right, they were not about to deny a principle as old as sin. They did mean —and while I put their implications into more modern language, I do not believe I distort them—to ask whether they as Jews did not compromise their belief in the one God by paying taxes and thus acknowledging the sovereignty of a worshipper of false gods. This problem, they thought, could not have occurred to Alexandrians or Antiochenes or Ephesians because they had no religious beliefs to protect.

The questioners are identified as Pharisees and Herodians by Mark and Matthew; Luke's "scribes and high priests" may be ignored as the statement of a man who did not know. Pharisees and Herodians in general had little enough to do with each other; it would not be the last time that opposing factions were united against a common enemy. In politics, as I have noted above, there was no "Pharisaic" position, but nothing we know about them would make it impossible for them to cooperate in this essay in dialectics. "Herodians" seems to designate not only courtiers ("hangers-on"?) of Herod Antipas, but members of a party who believed in and worked for a restoration of the satellite kingship of the Herodian house over the former domains of Herod the Great, detached from his son Archelaus and divided among different administrations responsible to the legate of Syria in 6 A.D. It can be said safely that the members of this group would at once have reported to the Roman authorities a negative answer to the question; this incident occurred during the reign of Tiberius, during which the practice of "tattle-tale" (Latin *delatio*) had become quite common and quite rewarding. The Pharisees should not have shared this interest; it is still a disputed question how many of the Pharisees were hostile to Jesus. The question as described was an obvious trap; no answer was possible which would not give great offense to someone, and which would not align Jesus with some party or parties at the cost of the enmity of some other parties. All in all, the question and the situation of the dialogue contain nothing improbable. To appreciate the situation, one needs only to imagine (or to remember) a modern meeting at which the speaker is asked for a flat Yes or No on such questions as busing or abortion.

Jesus asked for and was given a Roman coin. The Romans, always realists, did not accept payment of taxes in any of the exotic coinages minted by satellite kings and city-states; they wanted something they could trust. Jesus asked whose picture was on the coin. Jesus did not wish to enter a discussion of political philosophy. Coinage is an act of sovereignty if anything is. One of the first things the Zealots did when they rebelled against Rome 35 years later was to mint their own coins. Our own "sovereign" states, 50 in number, are not allowed to exercise sovereignty by minting their own coinage, although some of them are much larger than many sovereign states. But they never mint coins nor issue stamps, although they do collect taxes. As I said, Jesus entered neither there nor anywhere else a discussion of political philosophy. As plainly as any words could have said, to hold the coin aloft was to answer the unspoken question of who is boss.

Furthermore, it said clearly without words that you, by

using this coin, accept the sovereignty which it proclaims. You have already answered the question which you ask; for if you acknowledge Caesar's sovereignty, you certainly acknowledge his right to impose and to collect taxes. Jesus said none of these things flat out; that would have wounded Jewish sensibilities. He let the coin do the talking. As the report of the conversation goes, the coin spoke loudly and clearly enough to terminate the conversation. There are times when a conversation or a dispute is ended, when someone utters the last word; this account tells of one such episode.

The saying, "Give Caesar what is his and give God what is his," does not answer the question. If Jesus meant, "The coin is Caesar's; it has his name on it; give it to him," he still did not answer the question: is it "right"? This is the kind of evasion which Jesus makes only to such questions: answer the question yourself, or recognize the answer you have already given. The answer says nothing, because it refuses an answer to the impossible question: what belongs to Caesar and what belongs to God? That question Jesus has left the questioners to answer for themselves. It is difficult for me to figure out how Jesus could have divided the reality of human existence into areas which belong to God and to Caesar respectively and exclusively. This could be criticized as an unforgivable lack of precision in an area where precision is esteemed to be of the highest importance. But I did not create the phrase nor am I trying to make it the basis of a Christian political philosophy. No doubt it could be suggested that Jesus meant that one should give to Caesar what God has committed to him; this was thought of a long time ago, and it is the theory of the divine right of kings (and of other forms of government). This is the only thesis of medieval political theory which survives in modern politics. Jesus knew as well as anyone else that the claims of God and Caesar are both totally and mutually exclusive, and that in the projected division Caesar will allow God nothing which Caesar wants. Jesus did not say this, possibly because even the Herodians might have caught something that explicit. Someone did catch it; this saying has become, in the admittedly garbled reports of a garbled trial scene, a saying that taxes should not be paid to Caesar. To question the exercise of governmental authority is, in the minds of governments, to deny it. I think Jesus knew as well as we do that in any question of what is due to God and what is due to Caesar the government will make the decision, feeling sure that God will not assert his power to the contrary.

Other sayings which may be adduced do not touch the question of politics as directly, and thus may be the more easily dismissed as irrelevant, or are doubtfully the authentic words of Jesus, and thus may be questioned as not really expressive of his mind, or are limited by the archaic cultural background in which they were spoken and therefore not pertinent to the questions of contemporary humanity; why should the political theology of the New Testament say any more to us than the cosmology of the New Testament? I shall try to take account of these and related problems in discussing the sayings which I adduce. And certainly that saying which most clearly refers to the political world in which Jesus lived is found in Mark 10:42-45; Matthew 20:25-28; Luke 22:25-27. Like the previous saying, this is attested in all three Synoptic Gospels. The variations in form are greater but not significant for the meaning of the saying. Naturally I am inclined to regard this as an authentic saying of Jesus because it is certainly grist for my mill, and there is no use in pretending that I am entirely dispassionate in my treatment of this passage.

All three versions agree that the saying was uttered in response to a dispute among the disciples about who were to be the greatest among them. Mark and Matthew identify two of the disputants as James and John, a detail which Luke has lost. There is nothing improbable about such a dispute, even though it was a dispute in a dream world; the disciples of Jesus have often enough entered such disputes in the last 1900 hundred years to make it credible that such a dispute arose in the original group of the Twelve. There is room for discussion about the degree to which the original saying may have been expanded to the form found in the present Gospels. Jesus resolves (or rather squelches) the dispute by drawing a contrast between the secular rulers of political societies and the behavior which he prescribes as proper to his disciples. He portrays (or is quoted as portraying) the holders of secular political power in quite abusive language; modern translations which use such phrases as "lord it over them" or "make their importance felt" (throw their weight around?) catch the flavor of the original Greek. Luke adds a note of sarcasm which is almost certainly not original but is faithful to the spirit; he makes fun of the title "benefactor" (Greek *euergetes*) which Hellenistic rulers commonly added to their titulary. Jesus says there shall be none of that among you; you shall vie with each other only in seeing who can give the most and the lowest service to others. The highest rank should be the lowest slave; this was uttered in a culture in which "slave" was an operative social term. No doubt it is out of reverence to this text that the Roman Pontiff includes in his titulary *Servus servorum Dei,* slave of God's slaves. I thought of this the first time I saw Pope Pius XII borne into St. Peter's on a portable throne accompanied by fans of ostrich plumes, part of the insignia of royalty of the ancient Egyptian Pharaohs. It seems that the lowest of God's slaves found some even lower slaves to carry his chair on their shoulders.

If one thinks that Jesus was saying, or that the scribes who composed this dialogue intended to represent him as saying, "Look, you people are going to establish a church in my name and I do not want that church to show any of the signs or the reality of that kind of power you see in things like the Roman Empire," that one totally misunderstands the saying. The intention of Jesus to found a church or to have his disciples found a church is hardly the clearest feature of the Gospels, whether we are speaking about "the historical Jesus" or "the risen Jesus" or "the triumphant glorified Christ." The present verse has no clear reference to any ecclesiastical body then existing or planned to exist. It says simply that the disciples are not to exercise political power as it was exercised in the world of the time, and if anything in particular is the target, it is the pomp which is always associated with power. Someone wrote in recent years that the dress of the most powerful ruler in the world is a business suit; I may have written it myself. If that is true, let me add that no one could mistake the President of the United States for anyone else. Jesus wants no pomp or display or throwing of weight among his disciples. If they get into lines of work where this is thought to be necessary, they will have to behave as if they were not his disciples. And one begins to wonder how much pomp and bullying is demanded by the exercise of authority. As far as the members of a church which claims to bear his name and to continue his mission exhibiting pomp and power and lording it over the disciples, one can say only that Jesus has already spoken to that. Jesus is no more sympathetic to the exercise of power and the symbols of power than he is to wealth. And if he were sympathetic, this saying cannot be authentic.

We then run into the question of how Jesus designated his mission and himself. The question has enough complexity to satisfy even the most eager seeker after complexity, and I state my views with all humility and all due reservations that I may be totally wrong. But even if I am wrong about the meaning of the phrase "reign of God" and the title "Messiah" (Christ), I do not believe the general thrust of my thesis (for that is what it is) is seriously weakened by what may be an error in detail; of course it is not strengthened. It would be seriously weakened if it were shown that these words were used by Jesus with clear and unmistakable political implications. As far as I know, such an interpretation is not proposed by any modern scholar.

I may say of the reign or the kingdom of God ("heaven" in Matthew) what I have said about other things: if Jesus did not call his mission the proclamation of the reign of God, then we know nothing at all about what he said. It can be discussed—but will not be discussed here—whether his disciples were entirely faithful to his proclamation when they turned it into a proclamation of Jesus as the one in whom the reign of God came. Modern translators prefer to translate "reign" rather than "kingdom"; I am not sure why, but I accept their preference. The kingship of God in the Old Testament seems to mean clearly the power which puts an end to all politics; that power may be thought to be political or non-political or super-political depending on how preoccupied one is with finding a political meaning in everything. I will surprise no one who has followed me with any attention thus far when I say I find the reign of

God in the Old Testament to be the end of politics as we know it, and that the reign of God is nothing like the reign of human beings over each other and will not permit human beings to reign over each other. I say this fully aware of the contentious character of this statement, aware also that it is as defensible as any other interpretation of the eschatological reign of God which appears in the Old Testament books. I know also that the idea of the reign of God is complicated in some passages by the idea of the reign of his saints. I do not know that this means that his saints become the instrumens of God's rule. Whatever the phrase is taken to mean, it is clear that the words attributed to Jesus are free of any implications that the reign of God is also the reign of his saints.

What about the twelve thrones promised the twelve disciples in the "new age" (Matthew 19:28)? This promise is found only in Matthew and not in parallels in Mark (10:28-31) and Luke (18:28-30). Matthew exhibits a peculiar and not friendly interest in the Jewish religious establishment which is not shared by Mark and Luke; a promise that the disciples shall be enthroned upon this establishment expresses a hostility found elsewhere in Matthew. Such an enthronement cannot be regarded as political or secular in any sense. I believe therefore that I may treat it as irrelevant to my point. I trust this will show that I am not above using redaction criticism where it serves my purpose.

That the phrase "reign of God" had political implications for many of those who heard Jesus's proclamations of the reign seems to be generally accepted by modern scholars. Since men and women find political implications now in just about anything which will bear them, I see no reason to think that people were that much different then.

If the rather abundant literature called "apocalyptic" is any guide to popular belief (I am not sure that it is), we are quite safe in concluding that the reign of God to many, if not to most, Jewish listeners meant that God is going to put the Romans (and other heathens) in their place and put us, his chosen people, in our place, which is at the top of the heap—and God knows we have waited long enough. I am not quite sure that most Galilean villagers thought of this when they heard that the reign of God is near. It seems that many did; did not Jesus owe it to himself and to them to make it quite clear that the reign of God was something else altogether? Otherwise, whatever the Romans did wrong, they did Jesus no injustice—as Brandon more or less said.

My purpose in this book is to show that Jesus did make it clear—so clear that we Christians refuse to believe it. I quoted Vincent Taylor above in another connection and applied his words to a problem to which he did not apply them, and I repeat it here: this is what Jesus said, this is what Jesus meant—the Reign of God is totally apolitical; and with all due reverence we abandon him. It is worth noticing that the problem troubled someone in the first century some years after Jesus had died. The question is raised in the conversation between Jesus and Pilate (John 18:33-38). With all my colleagues I find it impossible to believe that this conversation ever took place. We have no assurance that it even echoes something Jesus actually said at another time and in another context. It does show that when the Gospel of John was written the Romans wondered (or some Christians thought the Romans wondered) whether Jesus himself or those who preached him had been or were engaging in political (meaning subversive) activity. John places the explicit denial of this in the mouth of

Jesus, and he represents Pilate, the Roman officer directly concerned with the case, as satisfied with the denial of Jesus. It shows also that the author of the Gospel (and presumably those for whom he wrote his Gospel) believed that they were faithful to what Jesus was and said in creating this dialogue. We should not think that the Gospels created sayings and dialogues just as the authors desired and needed them.

Is this dialogue faithful to what we know of the mind of Jesus (assuming that his mind can be known)? My discussion of the "political" passages suggests that it is as faithful as the authors knew how to be. Jesus was no threat to Rome as Rome understood threats. Of course it was quite impossible for the Roman Empire to maintain itself if it were administered by authentic Christians on authentic Christian principles; but the Romans did not know that, and neither did the author of the Gospel of John. Neither did the doubtfully authentic Christians who began to administer the Roman Empire after Constantine. I do not believe that either the Romans of the first century or the author of the Gospel of John ever foresaw the unlikely possibility that authentic Christians would some day take charge of the Empire, and they were right: it never happened. Martin Dibelius in an article written many years ago said that only a few Christians and a few Roman administrators perceived the deadly, irreconcilable opposition between the Roman way of life and the Christian way.[1] I suppose this article, read many years ago, influenced my view of the "deadly, irreconcilable conflict" of which I write. Among the Romans Dibelius included Diocletian, who was responsible for the only serious effort made by the Roman government to destroy Christianity. We may be grateful that Diocletian has had no successor in the United States; but is existing Christianity a real threat to the American way of life? "The irrepressible conflict" which Diocletian saw was resolved when Rome became Christian and the Church became Roman. Each party gave up more than they knew when they embraced each other. I find I am simply restating my conviction that Christianity is apolitical and that up to this point in history every effort to politicize it has been disastrous for Christianity. So lest I belabor the point unto tediousness (I may have already done so) let us turn our attention to some other sayings of Jesus which may touch the question.

One such "saying" is found in the temptation story (Matthew 3:8-10; Luke 4:5-8). It is unnecessary to say (but I do say it) that this is not the report of an actual conversation, so I really do not know how much I can make out of the point that the answer which Jesus is represented as making to the tempter is not a flat denial that the kingdoms of the world and their power and glory are his to give. The thought behind the story seems to be that Satan offers something he can deliver. In plain language the kingdoms of the world lie in the domain of Satan, and Jesus will have nothing to do with them. If one believes, as I do, that Satan is a quite fictitious non-reality who is the image of something quite real, one may ask what is the reality to which the kingdoms of the world belong. As long as I stick to exegesis I do not think I can carry the question any farther. One is reminded of Augustine: "Without justice what are governments except big robber gangs?" Governments have historically lacked justice more frequently than they have exhibited it; and I think the mythological Satan may say quite legitimately that robber gangs work for him.

There is a question of political implications in the use of

the words "Messiah" (Greek *Christos*) and "son of man"
as titles of Jesus. I think I may be excused from adding
to the enormous mass of literature which has been accumulated about the meaning of these words, especially
since I have nothing to add. Nor can I settle long-standing
controversies. Some degree of uncertainty must remain;
and while I shall try to lean on nothing which does not
have a large or, in most questions, a majority opinion of
modern scholars to support it, this uncertainty does cast
some doubt upon at least this portion of my thesis. The
word *Messiah* transcribes a Hebrew word which means
"anointed." In the Old Testament it means either a priest
or a king, each of whom was ritually anointed to inaugu-
rate his office. I pass the question whether originally the
king was also a priest—indeed, *the* priest. Both are often
called "the anointed one of Yahweh" to designate the
sacred character of their office. The use of the word to
designate an expected future savior is post-biblical (meaning here the Hebrew Old Testament).

I perhaps over-simplify when I say that the expected
future savior was thought of as a scion of David who
would restore the kingship (hence he is also called "son of
David," a title which in the Gospels is sometimes applied
to Jesus). The restored kingdom would be an establishment in which Yahweh would reign supreme over all nations, and his chosen people Israel, under their chosen
king, the new David, would share in the universal reign of
Yahweh. This reign would establish peace and prosperity
over all the earth; all enemies would either submit or be
destroyed. I believe it can be said that the Messiah of popular Jewish hopes was a national, patriotic and political
hero. This is to to say that the expected messianic reign was
inextricably linked with the political fulfilment of the peo-

ple of God as supreme over all other peoples. This summary I have tried to write carefully, knowing that there is no detail which will not be questioned by my colleagues; but I believe that while it may sin by brevity, it is not a distortion of history.

My thesis embarrasses me as a Christian because the name of the faith I profess shows that the followers of Jesus accepted for him the title of Messiah [Christ], whatever he himself may have said about it. If I say that Jesus transformed the meaning of the title "Christ," I shall have set myself an impossible task. But I cannot avoid the discussion. We may begin with the question which John the Baptist is said to have addressed to Jesus (Matthew 11:2-11; Luke 7:18-28). The question is not found in Mark, which removes it from one of the two major sources about the sayings of Jesus. This does not mean that we may not attribute the saying to Jesus; but if anyone questions us, we are in for an argument which we would not have if the saying were also found in Mark. It suits my purpose whether it is an authentic saying or whether it is an effort to interpret the mind of Jesus. I am not certain that this is a question which surely must have been addressed to Jesus, whether by John the Baptist or by someone else; but, as we shall see, there is more than sufficient evidence that the question arose and that Jesus actually spoke to it. So what did he say?

The fact that the earliest Christian writer (Paul) applies the title to Jesus suggests that Paul had some reason to think that Jesus accepted the title, or at least that it suited him. The fact also remains that the transformation of the meaning had already occurred when Paul used it; in his writing the title has no nationalistic, patriotic or political significance. Jesus has become a non-Jewish savior, and I

suppose I may suggest that this is at least one of the
reasons why Jews have not accepted him as a savior figure.
But it is very hard—if not impossible—to show that the
Gospels reflect the same transformation, although the
Gospels were written at least a generation after Paul. So I
ask again: what did Jesus say? And I may add: if what he
said was all that clear (a straightforward affirmation or
denial), the writers of the Gospels either misunderstood it
or concealed it.

The question of John is: "Are you he that is to come, or
do we look for another?" "He that is to come" (a phrase
which gave the late Sigmund Mowinckel a title for the most
important study of messianism in the last century or two) is
a circumlocution for the Messiah. Jesus answers (or is said
to answer) neither yes nor no, but recites a number of
miracles worked by himself and the proclamation of good
news to the poor, and adds a warning not to be offended
by this. The quality of this answer makes it all but certain
that it was not given by Jesus himself to any real question,
but by his disciples in answer to a Jewish question about
his messianic identity with the clear implication that Jesus
does not fill the bill. The answer is indirect with an equally
clear implication that this is the only Messiah that God is
going to send. I admit that this may be reading more
subtlety into the answer than the text has; but I am not sure
we should assume easily that the authors of the Gospels
were incapable of subtlety. The answer does show that
Jesus was recognized by his early followers not to fulfil
popular messianic expectations, and that these expectations, not the reality of Jesus, were what needed revision.
In this or any other explanation, the answer attributed to
Jesus (or manufactured for him) is a fairly clear denial of
any claim to be the national, patriotic and political
Messiah.

The confession of Peter is reported in all three Synoptic Gospels (Mark 8:27-30; Matthew 16:13-20; Luke 8:18-21). What was in Peter's mind we cannot tell; we can deduce it from the immediately following episode in which Peter objects to the announcement of a suffering and dying Messiah. In all three Gospels the confession of Peter is followed by an injunction not to reveal this (the "messianic secret"). It seems that we are here dealing with some prophecies *ex eventu* and probably therefore with a heavily reconstructed dialogue between Peter and Jesus. If Peter did blurt out such a confession, the Gospels report that it was immediately corrected by a declaration of the messianic reality of Jesus put in such clear terms that Peter rejected it. The element of authenticity in this passage is quite difficult to discern. It is clear that however its authenticity is to be judged, it is in no way a tacit acceptance of the national, patriotic and political Messiah. By the time this saying was written any association of Jesus with the Messiah was immediately associated with his passion and death. That Jesus himself made this association in this or similar dialogues is less clear; it is evident that I am uncertain about the authenticity of the "triple prediction" of the passion and death of Jesus. The question again is whether the authors of the Gospels and their sources were faithful to the remembered words of Jesus when they made the association.

The entry of Jesus into Jerusalem (celebrated in the liturgy of the former Palm Sunday) is reported in all four Gospels (Mark 11:1-10; Matthew 21:1-9; Luke 19:29-39; John 12:12-15). Setting aside the note that the Gospel reports may exaggerate the tumult aroused by this display, it is certain that this was a reenactment of Zechariah 9:9 and would have been recognized as such by all the spectators if they knew their Bible as well as we seem to think they knew it. If they did, they would also recognize that the king who comes there is described not only as "a righteous savior" but also as "meek," the same word we have referred to above as designating the oppressed and the poor. Such a display could only have been deliberate, and that is the way the Gospels describe it; it was planned by Jesus himself. It was a statement by visual display, and it said, "Here is your Messiah." If it were not for the high seriousness which is supposed to pervade all discussions of theology and politics (theopolitics?), the unwise might say that Jesus was making fun of the Messiah; and we know that Jesus never made fun of anything, did he? One may wonder whether the story, in spite of its massive attestation, really relates an actual event; this question I cannot settle. If it does, it adds another instance in which Jesus rejected the political Messiah.

The three Synoptic Gospels attest that Jesus solemnly professed his identity as the Messiah in his judicial hearing before the supreme council of the Jews (Mark 14:55-64; Matthew 26:59-66; Luke 22:66-71). There are genuine problems about the historical reality of this process, and I shall not attempt to go into them. I may notice that according to the Gospels no disciple was among those present, even as a spectator. In all three Gospels Jesus adds to his affirmation an allusion to the heavenly coming of the Son of Man (Daniel 7:13-14). We are not, of course, dealing with a report of the actual words of Jesus, if this transaction ever occurred; but the saying rather clearly limits any claim of Messiahship to an eschatological claim. This is the only claim which Jesus was in a position to make; this does not show that he made it. One may believe that at this moment when Jesus was abandoned and beyond all human help he might have said, "Yes, I am your Messiah and there will not be another," but I do not know that he said so. I am not trying to settle this exegetical question. I am satisfied that if there was a moment in the life of Jesus when the claim to be the national, patriotic and political Messiah would have been not only vain, idle and ridiculous, it would have been fatuous, that was the moment. And since I believe that Jesus avoided being vain, idle, ridiculous and fatuous, I do not believe that he made such a claim at that time. It is probably safe to say that such a claim would have been all these things at any time. He claimed that his mission was to proclaim the arrival of the reign of God; this he had done, this he was doing, and this he continued to do until the end.

We may turn now to sayings which are clearly attributed to him and which have every chance of representing something he said; the point made in them is clear enough to make the question of whether they are exact quotations mere piddling. The first set deals with general principles which should govern interpersonal relations. By accident I read during the composition of this chapter a passage in a book by Walter Kaspar which says something I have long felt like saying, and it can be applied to these texts as well as to where he applies it: "Why should we attribute less originality to Jesus than to some hypothetical post-Easter prophet, whose name we do not even know?"[2] These passages are all found in collections of sayings of Matthew 5:38-48 + 6:14-15 + 18:21-35; Luke 6:27-36. These well-known texts deal with the forgiveness of enemies, the bearing of offenses, the reconciliation of enmities, the renunciation of violence and general recommendations which can be paraphrased as recommendations to be the world's patsy. Has no one noticed that in the exchanges of normal daily life it is much easier and more agreeable to deal with

patsies than it is to deal with those with whom every encounter is a duel? I am ready, of course, for the stock
answer that these are commendations for personal and
private morality, which is a matter of personal choice (!),
and that matters of public policy must be judged by quite
different canons. If that be the case, then Jesus said
nothing relevant to public morality or public policy, and
the Christian theololgian should not intrude into the discussion. Is this what is meant by the autonomy of the secular? Public morality and public policy are to be formed as
if the Incarnation had never happened, and I am safe in
repeating that the state is not an object of redemption. The
state is one of the consequences of sin, like disease, con-
cupiscence and mortality. During the writing of these
chapters the United States bishops have issued two joint
pastoral letters on peace and the economy which come
close to denying the autonomy of the secular.

It is obvious that most of the sayings in this collection
would, if applied to the relations of states with other states
or the government of their citizens or subjects (in this
context what is the difference?), either destroy all existing
policies or make it impossible to execute them. The
name of the game in international relations is "legitimate
national self-interest"; you can see this stated explicitly
and implicitly in the op-ed page of the latest Sunday news-
paper. It happens to be for me the *Los Angeles Times,* but
in this feature the *Times* shows no difference from other
metropolitan newspapers which have been my regular fare
at different times during the last 60 years. In this respect
Democratic and Republican newspapers as well as liberal
and conservative newspapers do not differ from each
other. In that period of 60 years it may have happened a
few times that legitimate national self-interest would have

been served by bearing offenses, forgiving injuries, offering reconciliation to those whom we thought our national enemies, by going the second mile and turning the other cheek. If anyone can think of such recommendations made either by public officers or by journalistic commentators, I shall be grateful to be told about them, and I will owe an apology to the public officers or to the journalists whom I have neglected, or to their memories if they have passed from our midst. A recent president, nearly canonized by his admirers, summed up his own politics as, "Do not get mad; get even." It is safe to say that a public officer who did not put legitimate national self-interest at the absolute top of his priorities would be called a traitor to his trust. And it is the government which determines the legitimate self-interest.

I remember being associated with a group which wished to undertake the sending of a shipment of medicines to Viet Nam, recently devastated by our bombing attacks. The Department of State refused permission. I kept for some years (but lost in one of my moves since then) a copy of the letter we received from a Mrs. Margaret Leighton, which in the tones of a schoolmistress, denied the permission to send the material because of the great possibility that it would fall into the hands of our enemies (with whom several presidents had assured us we were not at war). Mrs. Leighton did not discuss the reasons why more care was exercised in the dropping of medicines than in the dropping of bombs. If Uncle Sam has enemies, do not you make any effort to forgive them, reconcile them or assist them in their needs, even if they are non-combatants injured by our generous distribution of high explosives. When you get the knife in, twist it. I thought of writing a letter to the Undersecretary of State for whom Mrs.

Leighton wrote (a Mr. W. deV. Katzenbach, now forgotten), but I refrained; what good would be served by telling him or Leighton that they were bastards when they were only doing what they were paid to do? For the first time in my life the government of the United States, in a direct encounter, forbade me to act like a Christian; and I do not get such impulses often enough to let someone stand in the way.

The same or similar problems would arise about the administration of internal affairs. If people began to seek reconciliation and forgive offenses, most of the members of the legal profession would be deprived of a lucrative living, which is based upon carefully nurtured quarrels. Paul, whom I have avoided quoting (although he has often been thought to be an excellent interpreter of the mind of Jesus), wrote to Corinth that Christians who went to law with each other acted like unbelievers (1 Corinthians 6:1-11). I will be told that modern life is much more complex than I think; but Corinth of the first century had risen more than somewhat above the level of Neanderthal man. I shall steal again a phrase from Edmund Burke and say that complexity is the last refuge of scoundrels. It is not clear to me that the complexity of modern civilization has rendered forgiveness and reconciliation archaic modes of living in society, or that many problems arise which would not be solved by these archaic methods.

The statement of the renunciation of violence as a means of dealing with other people is clear enough; Christians have never questioned either that Jesus said it or that it admits no qualification. Christians, except for a few eccentric sects like the Friends, the Mennonites and the Church of the Brethren, have simply decided that they cannot live according to these sayings of Jesus. To put it more accurately, they have decided that they do not wish to live according to these sayings. Whatever one may think about the orthodoxy of these churches concerning such doctrines as the number and nature of the sacraments, justification by faith and by works, the nature of the priesthood, the primacy of the Roman Pontiff or the monarchical episcopate, even conservative Roman Catholics must grant that these churches have grasped the true meaning of what Jesus said about violence better than Catholics or any other mainline church. I am sure that members of these churches have heard often enough that they live under the umbrella of the United States Defense establishment and of state and local police which they on principle reject. Let me say that I have noticed that the Mennonites tend to withdraw from urban conglomerations and live quite successfully apart from local police protection at least as peaceably as those who live in the lap of such large and well-run police departments as those in New York and Chicago. The local police are not protecting anyone from the members of the peace churches. They ask for no special protection from the United States Defense forces and would be quite willing to live defenselessly if they were allowed. They have proved orderly, industrious and law-abiding citizens. If others let them alone as they let their neighbors alone, there would be no need for police. I do not praise them entirely for this, as I do not praise the early monks, because Jesus did not withdraw. If the Roman Catholic Church were to decide to join the Mennonites in refusing violence, I doubt whether our harmonious relations with the government would endure the day after the decision. Yet we Catholics know that the Mennonites are right.

Without violence governments would have no power to

impose their will upon their own citizens or upon the citizens of other countries. Without violence governments could not impose their laws upon their own citizens, good laws as well as bad laws; and only the government can decide which laws are good and which are bad. Personal moral judgment—conscience—has no standing before the law, which forms my conscience for me, as it did for the medicines intended for Viet Nam. I will be told that personal conscience would turn life in society into chaos. Without asking what anyone thinks it is now, I will say that Jesus must have had something like this in mind when he said, "To Caesar what is Caesar's, to God what is God's." Did he imply that in public life there is something that is not God's? This implication must be understood by those who accept Stephen Decatur's toast, "My country right or wrong," and submit to the government's dictates of conscience. In the same way, a society which allowed itself to be governed by the bearing of offenses and the forgiveness of enemies and which showed itself yielding rather than competitive would paralyze its entire legal, commercial, industrial and mercantile structure. We cannot do this and we cannot allow it to be done. It is because of this vast and many-faced opposition between the sayings of Jesus and all the principles by which civilized society lives, moves and has its being that I ask whether Christianity and western civilization can ever be reconciled. One of them must die or change its character, which is a kind of death. If western civilization were thought of as existing in a world in which there were no competition and no domination and no exploitation, those who manage and share that civilization simply would not know what to do.

VI. SALVATION THROUGH WISDOM

*Has not God turned the wisdom of
this world into folly?*

—1 Corinthians 1:20.

I BEGAN this disquisition with the statement that I believe
that western civilization is in essential opposition to Christianity because the sayings of Jesus clearly rejected three of
the pillars of the structure of civilization. I have dealt with
civilization's cult of wealth and power, and it was not difficult for me to say what I meant. When I come to the third
essential component of civilization I find it hard to express
myself. It finally became clear to me that it is hard because
of the three demons it is the third demon which I myself
worship most devoutly and have worshipped all of my
adult life. This is the idol which in my innermost heart I
really do not wish to burn. Wealth I can pretend to dismiss—as long as someone near me has it; power I can pretend to dismiss—as long as those in power let me have my
own way. I fear I cannot write about the third demon even
with the conviction, however deep or shallow it is, that I
have shown so far about the first two. For the third demon
I have not even found a name; but if Mammon is the first
and Satan the second, I suppose Apollo would do as a
name for the third.

A few years ago I prepared an address which dealt in
general terms with some of the themes of this book. In
preparing this address I composed a paragraph which I
shall reproduce here nearly as I wrote it; I no longer have
the manuscript. It will help to identify that third demon
and serve as a springboard for my apostasy from his cult.

AN INTELLECTUAL'S PROFESSION OF FAITH

I believe in intellect. I believe that it is the highest faculty of the human person. I believe that it is the human mind that distinguishes us from those whom we call brutes and which makes us the image and likeness of God, as Holy Scripture calls us on its first page. I believe it is the human reasoning power which makes it possible for the Word of God to become incarnate, and for human beings to hope for a fulfilment which the Scriptures describe as being like to God, because we shall see him as he is. I admire the achievements of men and women in the arts and sciences, all of which are the achievements of intellect. I believe that the human being is capable of anything to which he sets his mind, and that there is nothing true, good or beautiful which lies beyond the grasp of the human mind, and that there is no element in the human condition which we cannot subdue to our legitimate aims and desires if we think about it.

When I first wrote this, I was trying to recapitulate what I have accepted as a fundamental principle of my own life for 54 years—or, to be precise, since the Jesuits introduced me to literature in 1930 and placed Newman's *Idea of a University* in my hands. The principles which Newman set forth so well—better, I think, than anyone else—stoked the flames for a life of half a century dedicated to the pursuit of learning, and left me with the conviction that this life never needs to be examined to see whether it is worth living. That conviction has been shaken. My profession of faith may sound, as I believe it is, somewhat secular. It certainly reeks of the snobbishness of the intellectual. But I had satisfied myself that this is one secular area where one need not fear the domination of the secular. The training I experienced included warnings that the occupational sin of the intellectual is pride; and of all the vices pride is the most diabolical, because it is the most spiritual. I took what measures I could to avoid at least the obvious manifestations of pride, which I took to be an unshakable conviction of the supreme importance of oneself; perhaps I avoided only the more obvious manifestations of vanity, but it is not my purpose to carry on an examination of conscience with my readers. I wonder whether a saying of Archbishop Ullathorne, a nineteenth century English prelate, may not be applied to scholars as a body, as well as it may be applied to the Jesuits, the Archbishop's original target. He said that the Jesuits were a body of men each of whom was individually humble, but they exhibited an overweening corporate pride.

Up to the middle of the eighteenth century the Jesuit education which I had received—and I have never regretted that I did not have another—assured those who had it of standing in the academic world. The very unpopularity of the Jesuits was an attestation that they were recognized as disciplined minds. In the twentieth century the Jesuit identity was no longer a substitute for any other degree. I remember a Protestant colleague, a good friend (now deceased), who once made some searching inquiries about my life and work in the Society of Jesus, of which I was still a member. I answered with some reluctance and something less than fullness, but what I said was enough to elicit this response: "You know, we Protestants have long been really afraid of you Jesuits. Those others (mentioning some old and respected orders) do not frighten us; but you do. I shall be glad to tell my Protestant colleagues, from what you have told me, that we need not be afraid of the

Jesuits.'' I am happy to say that the Jesuits, whose membership no longer includes me, have not lost their awesomeness as much as my friend thought. I tell this simply to show that membership in the Jesuits did not authenticate one as an intellectual in America. In fact, membership in the Catholic priesthood and in the Society were more of an obstacle to reaching authenticity than a help.

In spite of these and other obstacles (most scholars meet obstacles), I think I have earned my varsity letter as an intellectual. I have a modest but respectable bibliography of books and articles which are regarded as competent if less than great; I have a very small bouquet of tributes such as awards and honorary degrees and I have been president of the two major American societies of biblical interpretation. The honor of which I am most proud (vain, in fact) is the presidency of the Society of Biblical Literature in 1966, since it was the first time since its foundation in 1880 that this Society had elected a Roman Catholic to this office. There is a certain absence of ivy in my academic history, but I have been telling myself for years that no one ever heard of the University of Königsberg before or since Immanuel Kant.

In 50 years as a practicing intellectual in the Roman Catholic Church I have met my share of anti-intellectuals—sometimes I think more than my share, but I am sure some would dispute this. My greatest fear in writing what I am going to write is that I will sound like an anti-intellectual. There is no doubt that my views—unworthy of the name of principles—have changed, matured, broadened—or hardened and narrowed, like my arteries, or become rigid and unresponsive, like my nerves and muscles. I cannot be sure. I am consoled by the thought that most of my colleagues take criticism with some grace—often ill grace, but they know their duty. How kindly will they take criticism that suggests that the critic thinks their whole enterprise is rearranging deck chairs on the *Titanic?* As the ranting of an anti-intellectual, that is how they will take it. I fear they will not even listen while I say that they can do what the unlearned cannot do, and I wish very much that they would do it. Yes, I am going to criticize them as I have seen no one do it in my life, and it will be for not doing what only they can do.

Let us recognize, and I think it will pass without dispute, that western civilization has won its dominant position because of its intellectual quality. This is not to deny the values achieved by the intellect in other civilizations, such as the Indian and the Chinese; I cannot praise them or find fault with them because I do not know them. I believe I can say that I find their intellectual achievements no threat to my way of life, and I think they find the intellectual achievements of the West a threat to their way of life. Therein lies the difference. The artificial cult of the Orient among some members of western civilization is pursued with no expectation that these members of our culture will affect any real change in the direction of western civilization. They are faddists, and they know it. The future may prove me wrong and them right, but that future is so far away that they will not be here to rejoice at my discomfiture nor I to bemoan my error. I am convinced that western civilization has fastened its deadly embrace upon the surviving Asian civilizations. They have lost the battle of technology, and they have not realized that one cannot borrow or imitate technology without accepting a way of life and a way of thought.

I mention technology because I believe that technology is the first thing that comes to mind when one speaks of the intellectual dominance of western civilization. If one may apply a biblical figure, technology is the fruit of the tree of knowledge of good and evil, attractive to the eye and pleasing to the taste; but on the day you eat of it you shall die. Technology arises from the accumulation of over 5000 years of recorded wisdom and experience; when I say that you cannot buy, borrow or steal it unless you buy the whole package, I say something which I cannot prove. I can only ask you to think abut it. Let us compare it to the learning of a foreign language, which millions have done without special talent or training. When people learn a foreign language well, they become French, German, Spanish, Italian or whatever it is that they have not been; they learn to think, feel and respond like those who speak the language they are learning. Perhaps it is with some disgust that they realize that they cannot learn to speak this language unless they become one of these people.

It is not the tools of war that are destroying old and well established cultures, it is the tools of peace. When the Roman Empire "fell," the barbarians had no intention of destroying it; they wanted to become Romans. Becoming Romans beat sitting huddled around fires in the frosty plains of northern Europe, gnawing on raw meat. They even proved their *Romanita* by turning their languages into bastardized forms of Latin. A Roman poet exaggerated when he said that Greece took captive her ferocious captors; he did not think that Rome would do the same thing. I have mentioned that the Greeks could not teach politics to the Romans. Nor did they teach them the arts, at which the Greeks excelled and the Romans were not even good imitators. It took more than a thousand years for the descendants of the Romans to produce Botticelli and Michelangelo. As I said, I can do no more than ask my readers to think about it.

I do not mean that students of the western intellectual achievements must themselves go through a few thousand years of training. I do not know, for instance, how much the Japanese, the most successful students of western technology, have had to become western. Perhaps no one except the Japanese are capable of discussing this; and perhaps they would have to cease to be Japanese to discuss it. Only they themselves, I think, would be able to tell how much of accepted and traditional Japanese values, ways of thought, ways of responding to challenge and (let us not fear the word) morals have been renounced and replaced in order to adapt their culture to the production of motor cars, cameras and computers. Of course these skills can be learned; the question is what else must be learned in order to acquire them.

The professional intellectuals, of whom I am one, are the custodians, the expositors and the heirs of the traditional system of ideas and values upon which the structure of modern technology rests. The intellectuals are found in the academic world, for many of them are teachers and scholars. They are found in the world of literature, including the world of journalism. They are found in the traditional "learned" professions, law, medicine and divinity. If anyone suggests that members of these professions are often technicians rather than learned, I would remind them that there are as many technicians in teaching and scholarship as there are in medicine, law and divinity. This is said with all due respect to technicians, many of whom know their skill (and their limitations) superbly. They could give lessons in professionalism to many members of the aforementioned learned professions.

Intellectuals are also found (not often enough) in politics. Business and industry perhaps attract most of the talent, as Pitirim Sorokin pointed out fifty years ago; but those engaged in those occupations do not, I think, regard themselves as intellectuals nor are they so regarded by those who think that they themselves are intellectuals. This does not mean that those engaged in business and industry are not as smart and do not think themselves as smart as the intellectuals. One of the dozen sharpest minds I ever met was owned by a building contractor, very successful in the trade, who was a voracious reader. Intellectuals do not appear frequently enough in the arts, which explains why so much modern art does not even exhibit mechanical skill. To sum it up, they appear in all the areas of human endeavor which do the thinking and set the styles in living and doing. They are what an obscure Roman writer was called, the arbiters of elegance. In an era of bad taste, they create it. In an era of incompetence, they praise it. In an era of bungling, they say it went just as we planned it. They are proud as Satan, they are ferociously arrogant and snobbish, they spend a great deal of other people's money and they have much to answer for. My first criticism of my fellow intellectuals is that they do not do well the work which they insist that society overpay them to do, and that is thinking. Probably Larry Bird is paid more than any intellectual. Unlike them, he does his work so well that he is almost beyond criticism. He is a genuine professional who does superbly what he is paid to do. Plato would have liked him. I am not sure that Plato would think as well of most contemporary philosophers and critics.

My colleagues pay a vast amount of attention to trivia. We live in a period when any problem is met by the suggestion that a study be made; and studies generate more studies. These studies are made and filed, tons of them, but nothing is ever done with them. The study itself has become a substitute for action. Scholars are better students than doers; that is why we choose the vocation of scholarship. If the doers are referred to the studies, they will find them written in the dreary interminable prose which is part of the scholarly pose of objectivity. A scholar who can study starving children and remain objective should study something else. My own field, which I suppose is the particular area of theology which deals with biblical studies, I can illustrate from personal experience. I have counted words with the most diligent of my colleagues and done most of the things for which Browning's grammarian was praised at his funeral.

Probably the number of books and monographs published by theologians and exegetes which tried to explain the meaning of the Bible for life in the contemporary world has always been minimal compared to studies of the number of angels who can dance on the point of a needle; most of such studies are now made by sociologists, who, if they have not monopolized the study of trivia, have certainly developed the most imposing technique for it. My colleagues pursue with utmost finesse the sources of the sayings of Jesus, the thought processes of their redactors, the rhetorical techniques which lie behind their composition and the ways in which they responded to the needs of the earliest Christian communities. What I rarely hear from them is the way in which these sayings respond to the needs of the contemporary Christian community. My colleagues seem to have a paranoid fear of preaching, which may not be paranoid but well-founded in reality. I am not sure that a dedicated study of how the New Testament scribes have done their work should become a substitute for continuing the same work in a different place and time. Here as elsewhere the intellectuals do the thinking and set the styles. As a colleague now deceased once said of a celebrated

Notre Dame football team, they do all the running, all the passing and all the fumbling. And then we have the gall to complain because the preaching is done by Billy Graham and Norman Vincent Peale and the late Fulton Sheen; but Sheen at least had once been an intellectual.

I think my colleagues in theology and exegesis are open to the charge that they have become mandarins, who speak only to other mandarins about topics which are of interest only to mandarins in a style of discourse which is gibberish to any except mandarins, and one sometimes wonders about them too. The whole act may be a vast pretense, like the emperor's new clothes. How truthfully this charge can be laid against scholars in other disciplines I will let those scholars decide. It is popularly believed that doctors and lawyers deliberately cultivate gibberish in order to mask what they are doing (or failing to do) from the uninitiated. I still remember the shudder with which I heard a dentist describe a temporary condition which had come upon me as a "traumatic lesion." For this, I asked myself, did I devote the best part of eight years to the study of the languages of Horace and Sophocles, to hear nonsense uttered in Latin and Greek derivatives? I hoped that his knowledge of teeth rose above the level of his knowledge of languages. It must have, because my traumatic lesion was healed—or *natura sanavit seipsam,* for my medical readers, if I have any.

I do believe that the learned fraternity is in serious need of the art of communication by language to get back in touch with the simple faithful who pay their salaries and fees. Language among the learned fraternity has suffered a traumatic lesion, to borrow a medical phrase, and it is being treated by shrouding it in vapor. My low opinion of politicians has already been stated, and there is one thing I do not expect from contemporary statesmen; they will never do anything like the Gettysburg Address (318 words). If one of them did, the audience, drilled to expect the verbal flack of educated men, would ask in bewilderment, "What did he say?" Scholarship is or ought to be a form of public service and not a game like polo, which does not even draw large crowds, or an expensive enterprise dedicated to the production of a few more mandarins who can spend a leisurely life in the production of other mandarins. I hope this sounds angry and embittered. I can quote a recent issue of *Punch* and say: "The Bible has been good to me." I wonder whether I have been good to the Bible.

While the world of learning is a component of modern civilization without which modern civilization will not go, I wonder whether the world of learning is not a willing lackey of the other two demons, wealth and power. I may mention popular suspicions concerning the interest of physicians and attorneys in wealth; physicians and attorneys are well aware of these suspicions. It can be said in favor of my colleagues in other learned disciplines that although they are by definition smart enough to have become doctors or lawyers, they chose not to become doctors or lawyers and thus to move quickly into assured affluence. How many doctors, lawyers or divines have done what Albert Schweitzer did? There is a legend that he became a rather prickly character—possibly because he was reminded too often of his colleagues who would not touch what he was doing with a ten-foot pole. It is not dedication to the care and healing of the sick or the oath of Hippocrates which is responsible for the absence of doctors in urban slums and remote rural areas. I will be told that it is the lack of hospitals. I am so simple that I thought that physicians went where there are sick, not where there are hospitals. Jesus the healer never amounted to anything; he made house calls. The modern healer will never hear the words addressed to Jesus, "Sir, I am not worthy that you should come under my roof." I would not want my readers to think that I am unaware of physicians like Dr. Joseph Evans, who after retiring from a distinguished career went to South America to continue his practice, nor like the surgeon of Joliet, Illinois, who started a free clinic after retirement and was sued for malpractice. I am sure that my readers will be as happy as I to know that he stuck both the patient and her attorney in a countersuit. Were these two physicians average or even representative, the preceding paragraph should not have been written.

Divinity is not as obvious a path to affluence, but some have found ways. I never learned them—not because I did not want to, but just because I spent too many years with the Jesuits, who did not train their members in these skills. I visited a few Jesuit communities in Europe and the Near East where the level of daily living was appallingly low, and I owe it to my former colleagues to say this. Most divines do escape that kind of poverty; like the members of the other learned professions, they have some reason to worry about the public concern for their integrity.

No one in the academic world will admit that that world rewards its professionals excessively. I spent a few years at a famous university where the football coach was paid, I think, eight times what I received. It was a closely guarded secret what he did receive, and I was never asked to endorse any products on television, as he was. There are two things to be said to this. First, the football coach did not have tenure, as I did; two losing seasons would have him looking for employment elsewhere. Secondly, the football coach headed an enterprise which attracted over half a

million paying spectators to university events every year.
I may have been underpaid (I doubt it), but I do not think
he was overpaid. What Plato and Aristotle would have
thought of this I do not know. But when Plato went to
Syracuse to plan the government for the tyrant Dion, and
when Aristotle went to Pella to serve as tutor for Philip's
son Alexander, neither of them went to work for peanuts.
The tradition that scholars are hired guns may be as old as
learning itself, and it has included some venerable names. I
will steal from something I wrote, I think about thirty
years ago, without acknowledgement: when the revolutionaries of 1789 enthroned a harlot on the high altar of
Notre Dame de Paris as the goddess of Reason, their symbolism was better than they knew.

Scholars do not seek affluence; there are more promising careers than the pursuit of learning. Neither do they
fight it, with rare exceptions. The arts of technology,
which are supported by industry as well as by academia,
are the most attractive to scholars. Industry never lures
theologians or classicists. But apart from the windfalls of
industrial or government or foundation grants, the small
university or college town shows American living at its
gracious and beautiful best, far removed from the blight of
slums—which means the blight of the poor. These gracious
communities are not supported on peanuts either. The
scholar, even in the impecunious humanities, expects certain amenities: his office, his library, at least a shared sec-
retary, a sabbatical in which he may write monographs and
work on a book (intelligible to mandarins) and, he hopes,
in the course of years, a cottage in the mountains or at the
beach or at the lake. One cannot do serious work unless
one can get away from students and committees, can one?
In one of the *Eclogues* Virgil wrote: *deus nobis haec otia*

fecit, "God has granted us this leisure." For Virgil *deus* was Augustus; my contemporaries have other gods to thank. My tears for their plight are the tears of the crocodile.

Professors in modern academia have had to develop the new skill known as "grantsmanship." This is the derisive name given to the skill of presenting attractive proposals in writing and in personal interviews shown by ambitious scholars who desire to share in the seemingly unlimited funds available for research (those "studies" again) on any personal interest of the scholar which he can persuade the committee will advance the welfare of mankind, or more likely of some particular portion of mankind, or contribute to the world's store of socially useful information. The term "grantsmanship" is usually uttered by scholars who have been denied a grant. I fear there is more than a little dirty infighting in this area among scholars and their friends. Obviously I never received a grant except a sum to attend an International Congress of Jewish Studies in Jerusalem and present a paper (small as grants go). Men and women in my age group generally antedate the princely largesse of the foundations and the governments which bestow grants, and my criticism of "grantsmanship" may have a taste of sour grapes. But I have at times been struck by the easy assumption of some of my colleagues that they cannot take a sabbatical leave without a travel grant. Immanuel Kant never left Königsberg, as I remember, and he made a deeper impression on the world of learning than these my traveling colleagues will ever make. I intend to find fault with no one because he or she is not Immanuel Kant. I simply ask why, if they are not Kant, they cost so much more than Kant cost.

It would be petty of me to snipe at my colleagues in the profession of learning and the learned professions because so many of them seem to be at least as devoted to getting all they can while the getting is good as they are to the advancement and cherishing of knowledge and the teaching of the young. I have observed that such idols as Plato and Aristotle seem to have had their price; and I can now add Francis Bacon, the very patron of the modern advancement of learning. And I admit that I am being petty; I am more deeply concerned at their failure to criticize, in the proper sense of the word, the modern simple and uncritical faith in wealth as that good which meets all needs and supplies the fullness of human life. I would like to see scholars turn on that faith the weapons which unbelievers and agnostics have used against the no more simple and naive faith of religious believers. I feel this failure more intensely when I try to write about it because I find no colleague upon whose assistance I can lean and on whose wisdom I can draw to make sure that I am not swinging wildly at a vague and elusive target. Let me admit that I may have missed something important which is written right down my alley; I have not read everything and I do not pretend that I have. If I have missed something, the author, rather than feeling offended, will be grateful that another voice has been added to his or her own. But if such things have been published, the intellectual establishment has not given them the kind of attention which would have forced me to attend to them.

By criticism in the proper sense of the word I do not mean the random and ranting anti-wealth and anti-rich diatribes which are so easy to compose. If any readers think that I have heretofore demonstrated just how easy it is, I beg leave to assure them that I have written with a heavy restraining hand and have successfully withheld about 95 percent of the words which came to mind. By proper criticism I mean a restrained and rational evaluation of the place of wealth and the wealthy in our society, assigning to them their full values and granting the full recognition of their service—to use the hackneyed old word —to their fellow human beings as well as candid statement of the sins which must be laid to their responsibility. Such a balanced criticism cannot be written if one accepts the assumption that no human value can be achieved without wealth or the simplistic counter-assumption that humankind has no radical vice except the private ownership of property. There are six others I can remember. If I could turn some of my colleagues to set their talents and their learning, so far in excess of my own, to do this kind of work, I would feel that I had finally accomplished something worth while.

In particular, I would like to see them address the question: may men and women, singly or as a race, do whatever they are able to do? I do not know whether this question belongs to theology. When I raised it as a conversational football in a small gathering of Roman Catholic priest friends, I was surprised that the instant response was: why not? As the conversation developed, it turned out that no one really wanted to go that far; and a kind of consensus arose that except for restraints which a person or a group may impose upon themselves, human ability knows no restraints upon its power. This was the response of an intelligent, educated and sincerely religious group of men. I wonder whether it is a typical response of my contemporaries.

I think of two other possible responses, one drawn from literature and the other from theological reflection. The response from literature is what the Greeks called *hybris,* the kind of heedless pride and self-assurance which brought about a tragic collapse. I do not think that the authors of Greek tragedy believed that this invoked the wrath of the gods any more than I and my contemporaries do; Aeschylus, Sophocles and Euripides were not simple, unsophisticated minds. *Hybris* and the consequent *ate* (the curse) was something they thought to be a part of the human condition. As I have said of some other things, this observation cannot be demonstrated; if there is a possibility that it is valid, it gives us something to think about. We are not talking about moral law; we are talking about the abyss which faces humanity, singly or collectively, if human beings go too far. We never know how far that is until we have arrived and find that we have reached the abyss.

The second response from theological reflection is: if no limit is imposed upon human powers except the capacity of the human powers, how does man differ from God? When we say that God is omnipotent, do we not mean that he may do whatever he can do? Or if a reader rebels at that, will not he or she revise it to say that God may do whatever he wishes to do? And if men and women have that much power or well-founded hopes of reaching it, surely it is enough. If there is such a thing as theology and such a thing as God who is its object, my theological instincts rebel against a principle which identifies Man and God. This is really *hybris*.

We come, then, to the self-restraints imposed by men and women upon their power to do what they can. But on what principle do I impose such restraints? This, I suppose, has more to do than anything else with determining the kind of person I am. To commit this restraint to other persons entirely seems unreasonable; to refuse entirely any restraint from other persons seems, again, to be *hybris*. To accept restraints which I think nature imposes is to personify an impersonal reality; it is also to ignore the fact that civilized progress is mostly the history of the removal of what were thought to be restraints imposed by Nature. More profound knowledge of nature enabled humanity to remove those restraints. I may borrow a phrase from Niebuhr and say that I impose restraints upon my freedom to what I can do because of a sense of creatureliness. This is vague enough, and it leads to the question of morality as the moral will of God, which I have deliberately excluded from the discussion. Modern men and women must be assured that morality is more than imagined restraints of nature or established human conventions. So far no one has found a principle which keeps human beings from paving over more than ten percent of the surface of California, or staging motorcycle runs in the Mojave Desert, or filling the air with gasoline emissions, or manufacturing and distributing nuclear bombs. Morality does not do it.

The cult of Mammon cannot survive and flourish as it has flourished so long without a philosophical and theological undergirding which learned men and women have furnished it. The cult of wealth has always needed apologies for its failures, explanations for its cruelties, plans and techniques for doing what it wants to do constantly and, especially in the last two centuries, finding more efficient and more profitable ways to do it. Learned men and women, both within academia and outside it, have never been wanting to serve as its intellectual lackeys. I do not say—because I do not know—how much of this service has been rendered from genuine faith and devotion and how much has been rendered because the temple of Mammon rewards well those who serve it. There must be some genuine faith and devotion involved, because the esteem which Mammon has for its kept scholars is shown by the difference between the rewards of scholars and the rewards of moneychangers. The use of religious terms is not out of place because the devotion to wealth is not without a religious element. Just as a convinced Catholic author (or a convinced believer of any church) cannot write long without betraying how much that belief affects his thinking on all topics, so a convinced believer in the essential goodness of wealth cannot write for long without betraying how much that belief affects or governs his thinking. The essential goodness of wealth has innumerable skilled defenders who do not even give thought to their total devotion to the cause.

One would expect theologians who profess belief in Roman Catholicism, the church which venerates St. Francis of Assisi, to express some of the criticisms I have in mind. Some recent writers have expressed opinions on the amount of money involved in the papal budget. Such figures are as meaningless to me as interstellar distances; they are not accurate, and I see no need for quoting them. The figures impressed me less than the statement attributed to one archbishop that the figures were lower than the annual budget for his own archdiocese; and it was not the archbishop of Chicago, nor of any see in the United States. That the Roman Catholic Church thinks it needs money in large quantities to do the work of Jesus Christ, who had no money, has long been known. Unlike Jesus, those who work for the Catholic Church have no intention of being caught without a place to lay their heads. The commitment of the church to wealth and property—and to other owners of wealth and property—is obvious. I know of no restraint which the Church has exercised on its theologians who criticize—properly or improperly—the wealth of the Church, possibly because there have been so few to restrain. Liberation theology is quite another package; but

I shall get to that below. At this writing the United States bishops have released the first draft of a joint pastoral letter on the American economy. The final draft may be a moderate criticism of the cult of Mammon, which will be quite unprecedented.

I hesitate to give much space to those intellectual operations which can be summed up under the name of the arts. The first and very good reason for this reluctance is that I do not know enough about them, except the art of putting words together, to say anything which does not rise from profound ignorance. The second reason is that even if I could speak from some knowledge I am not sure that artistic criticism is a skill which should appear in a theological essay. Yet if I leave the arts completely outside theological examination it would suggest that there is no theological response to art, or at least that I should make no theological response. This does not seem to be tenable. I am a human being before I am a theologian. As a human being I have enjoyed at least some of the arts as much as my fellow human beings. I believe that as a paying spectator I am as much entitled to like or dislike the performance as any other ticket holder. May I say that I will assert as much freedom to respond to art as I assert in responding to dogmatic and disciplinary declarations of the Church. If one were to say that you have that freedom, but you should keep your theology out of your responses to art, I must ask in return how much ideology the artists insist that spectators and auditors leave out of consideration.

I have been a fairly diligent student of theology for 50 years, and theology is concerned with the human scene, as the arts are. When I go to the theater or the opera or the art gallery, I cannot pretend that 50 years of fairly rigorous intellectual work have not happened, or admit that I have not as much right to find the art relevant to my interests as the proponent of integration or social justice or feminism has to judge the art on its relevance to his or her interests. That because of our interests we may be thoroughly incompetent judges of art is irrelevant; art presents itself to the public and thus submits itself to the risk of public dislike, and nobody's freedom is under attack. Since I have spent some years in phrase-making, which has long enjoyed esteem as one of the fine arts, I have known some hostile reviewers. Some of them I thought were incompetent, but I never said so in public because I thought my sacred freedom to write what I wanted to write was matched by their sacred freedom to write that what I had written was junk. The freedom of the artist or the academician is not the only freedom in the world, nor is it the only freedom in danger.

This preface to my very few remarks on the arts as a component of western civilization went a little beyond what I intended. I may begin by returning to a fact previously observed: in Athens, which can claim to be the mother of the arts as well as the mother of democracy, the art like the freedom was enjoyed by only 14,000 adult males in a population over 100,000. We may wonder whether scholars have been the lackeys of the wealthy, but it is neither necessary nor possible to wonder whether the artists have been the lackeys of the wealthy. In modern democracies have the arts been democratized? Not as much as the motor car. Since the days of classical Greece and Rome the arts have been patronized and enjoyed by a very thin upper crust of extremely wealthy people. And why limit myself to Greece and Rome? The magnificent funerary art of ancient Egypt is found in the tombs of kings and nobles. That modern democratic governments have stripped the nobility of their palaces and converted the palaces into exhibition halls for art collected by nobles does not change the crude fact that the viewers who throng the Louvre and the Uffizi (I have been among them) are enjoying the contemplation of stolen goods. To paraphrase John L. Lewis once again, there is blood on those paintings, like the coal, the frest fruit and the coffee. I regret this deeply; can I reject Botticelli because he worked for the Medicis, or Michelangelo because he drew pay from the Renaissance Popes? The dedicated advocate of civil rights should say that I could not find a better reason for rejecting them. And so I come back to my thesis: even in the cultivation of beauty and the production of the most charming sights and sounds which the human genius has created western civilization has been unable to find a way to do the most innocent and wholesome deeds without exploitation of the human species. Art has never been produced for more than a few privileged scoundrels, and it is an accident when it reaches more than those few.

I think I have given some basis for my opinion that the intellect, the third pillar of modern civilization, leans heavily upon wealth, another pillar. We have now to consider the relations between the professional intellectuals and the power structure. I have already noticed that the alliance between the intellectuals and the politicians appears in Plato's post as adviser to the tyrant Dion of Syracuse, and I shall point out a few even more remote examples. The same Plato gave perhaps the earliest expression to the ideal which intellectuals have cherished ever since (I paraphrase his words roughly but I believe accurately): evils will never disappear from states nor from the relations between states until philosophers become kings and kings become philosophers. Put more crudely and in a more contemporary tone, the paraphrase might run: politics will always be run badly until we have government by experts. Plato had harsh words for those of his contemporaries who believed that the skills of rhetoric qualified one to manage the affairs of state. He called such men sophists and those skills the art of making the worse cause appear the better.

I have not tried to document this statement by examples because it does not seem necessary. Intellectuals have in modern times, if not throughout the course of what I have called western civilization, hovered on the fringes of power: the courts of kings and emperors, the halls of parliaments, the offices of cabinet ministers. If one studies the scribes of ancient Egypt and Mesopotamia, one sees these obscure and obsequious figures represented at the elbows, and I mean that literally, of kings and magnates. One knows that in an age when literacy was a rare and jealously guarded skill these scribes did not need the trappings of power; they were satisfied with the reality of power, and they retained the reality of power by never admitting that they had it. They were the first intellectuals, as far as we know, who were the hired guns (should we say hired pens or hired *styli?*) of political and economic potentates. If the art of writing were deemed to be the basic skill of modern civilization, then the scribe, the intellectual of his day, has always stood at the elbow of the men of power. One meets the modern successors of the scribes in the vast beehives of the offices of the federal, state and municipal bureaucracies. The modern scribes do not attempt to conceal their power, and they in no way cultivate obscurity and obsequiousness. It is more accurate to say that they flaunt their power. I may be charged with oversimplification if I classify as scribes both the internal revenue clerk and the Harvard professor who takes a leave from the university to head a cabinet department. Oversimplification is a charge which I have had to learn to enjoy; but in fact both the clerk and the professor are hired guns for Uncle Sam. They differ in their market price.

But the intellectual who accepts a commitment to public service—to use the customary euphemism—at least accepts a broader commitment than one who accepts a commitment to a particular party. It has always been hard for me to understand how my colleagues who zealously espouse political causes—and I do mean zealously, passionately—can pretend to maintain their pose of dispassionate and critical judgment and independent thought. In my experience nothing so narrows the vision and even blinds it and is so destructive of dispassionate and objective critical judgment as partisan politics. I find the dogmatism of partisan politics to be as narrow and intolerant as the dogmatism long (and not unjustly) identified with certain schools of Roman Catholic theology, and especially with the Roman Curia. I think I know this dogmatism and those who exhibit it fairly well; and it is not from hearsay that I find the same attitudes in party politics. I once subscribed to *The New York Review of Books* (this will surprise you). When the journal sent me a routine questionnaire about my nonrenewal, I answered that my intellectual life was not enriched by a journal written in the same broad liberal style and tone as the *Osservatore Romano*. To those who know *Osservatore* no explanation is necessary; to those who do not, to borrow a phrase, no explanation is possible. When I have somewhat endangered my career by refusing to submit to the thought control imposed by some officers of the Church of whose clergy I am a member, it seems stooping a bit to accept my marching orders in thought given me by a little clique of New York intellectuals. As a younger colleague recently said in a theological context, if it is not as clear as two and two are four, why is it taught as if it were?

I will risk imputing some motives to my colleagues who lend their time and their talents to partisan causes. Their plea, which they will immediately enter, is that they are not partisan causes; they are the causes of humanity, or of the poor and the helpless. Are they unaware that these causes have sheltered as many scoundrels as any other causes? Do they never ask themselves whether God or their causes really need them, or whether their presumably noble objectives can be achieved by other people and through other people and through other means? I ask for the basic humility to face the fact that those who differ from them may be just as sincere and just as intelligent and well educated as they think they themselves are, and to accept the possibility that these others may have thought of an equally good or even better way to do what they want done. I ask for the most basic humility of all, to borrow a phrase from an early "liberal" hero, in the bowels of Christ to think whether they might be wrong. And since I recognize that this is a request that partisan politics be replaced by civil rational discourse, the discussion will stop right here.

I believe—and not without cause—that the charms of association with power, with the persons found in centers where things are really done, the thrill of feeling that one has become a cog of a machine which can impose the will of its directors upon others, simply numbs the critical faculties which my colleagues usually exhibit. Political power does not offer anything so crass as wealth, and it does not need to. It has a beauty and a charm of its own, and it furnishes those who are associated with it the pleasure of knowing that others are compelled to follow their orders. In the ranking of human pleasures the pleasure of dominating one's kind must rank very close to the top. My imputation is that my colleagues who donate their talents and their services to partisan politics do so because they enjoy doing it, not because it pays well. Was it not one of our academics who said that power tends to corrupt? Generally the best and brightest of my colleagues cannot be bought with money except in very large quantities. You must offer them a chance to do what they think they do best, which is to manage other people's lives.

It is at this point that I must turn my attention to the recent movement in Roman Catholic theology called liberation theology. I take up this topic with some reluctance and not without some searching thought and self-examination, aided by the counsel of others. For I do not deny that my first encounters with this movement elicited from me a favorable response. I think some of my pages in earlier chapters show how liberation theology spoke to a number of ideas which I had been playing with for some years, although these pages may not show the number of years which went into this development. The reader may have assumed that I sound enough like liberation theologians to be one of them. I owe it to myself to declare quite clearly that I cannot accept some of the basic premises of liberation theology as I understand them; this proviso is not intended to be more than the usual conventional caution. God has given me an adequate set of wits which have not been retarded as badly as my ambulation, and liberation theology is anything but subtle.

I believe that liberation theologians will say that my refusal to accept their principles is due to a self-willed ignorance; that may be the kindest response they will give to my refusal. Saving their reverence, I may say that the first step in the process which led to my disillusionment was the discovery that as a group they are narrow, intolerant, dogmatic and incapable of sustaining criticism or even of entering into a rational discussion with those who differ from them, or even have questions about what they say. When I found they are as narrow as *The New York Review of Books,* I began to lose interest. My attitude was not changed even by the opposition of the Holy See to liberation theology; most of the time opposition from this source makes me antecedently sympathetic to any position. This is a confessed weakness in my habits of thought. In this instance two identical mindsets appeared to collide, and the only thing for me to do was to get out of the way, since I had no desire to be identified with either. Since the first drafts of this manuscript were composed it seems that the two mindsets were not as opposed as both sides thought, and that a reconciliation of the two may be in sight. By a strange perversity this makes my task of criticizing liberation theology more difficult, since my points of question are much the same as those made by the head of the Congregation of the Faith.

At this writing the Gospel of the Transfiguration occurred in the liturgy recently. In thinking over a homily something came to mind which I could not use in a homily, but I can use here. Three liberation theologians were present at the Transfiguration. One of them in rapture said, "Lord, it is good for us to be here. Let us make three tabernacles: one for you, one for Marx and one for Lenin." This parable is interpreted to mean that liberation theology is best called by a name which liberation theologians detest; it is an ideology. It is not a theology because it is not founded on the accepted theological sources—accepted, that is, by all Christian theologians, whatever be their sectarian differences. Their use of biblical theology is to my knowledge highly selective (I know everyone does it, but I am talking about liberation theology). Liberation theology dismisses as irrelevant, without any discussion, biblical elements which have as much title to consideration as the elements which they adduce as supporting their theses—for instance, the Exodus, which is clearly a non-event, and the holy war, which I have dealt with in an earlier chapter. I shall not enter into a full discussion of these elements; this would be another book which I am not writing.

I shall simply state some features of the theology which I am unable to digest, and I see no reason why I am obliged to make an effort to do more. Liberation theology is just one more theory of theological politics (theo-politics); it is not imposed upon me by an authority which I acknowledge, and I commit no sin against justice or charity if I reject it. I believe I am exercising no more than my due freedom in rejecting it, and I am not even obliged to state my reasons. In the interests of rational discourse I do state them; unlike liberation theologians, I invite criticism.

The reasons for my rejection can be discerned in the preceding pages of this book. The first of these is the assumption, hardly implicit, that human problems are due to the unequal distribution of wealth. This I believe is no more than a variant version of one of the three principles which I find essentially corruptive of western civilization, the principle that wealth is the essential good of human life from which all other goods flow. I have tried to make it clear that I believe that Jesus said that wealth is irrelevant to genuine human welfare, that no one is better for having it and no one is worse for not having any of it. I expect to have no more success in persuading liberation theologians of this feature of Christianity, which I think is essential, than I expect to have in persuading the wealthy—less expectation, in fact; the wealthy sometimes have a sense of guilt about their wealth, but a doubt of the righteousness of their theology has never crossed the mind of liberation theologians.

It is simply not true, as some have said, that the original sin of mankind is the possession of private property; this is pure ideology, unfounded in theology, history, economics or common sense. As a simplistic statement of how the reign of God is to be brought about its publication in allegedly serious writing astonishes me. I do not find that Jesus meant or said that you will surely overcome sin when you have a sufficient if frugal income, which sounds as if salvation comes from and is possessed by the middle class. Liberation theologians do not hear Jesus as criticizing the wealthy for their wealth, but only for having more than their share; I struggled with this problem in an earlier chapter. They hear him telling the poor that with sufficient wealth they can acquire the kingdom, that they have no faults except their poverty, for which they are not to blame. This I call highly selective interpretation.

My second reason for rejecting liberation theology is the absence of the theme of reconciliation, which I find dominant in the words of Jesus. Jesus even proclaimed the good news to the scribes and the Pharisees; he associated with prostitutes and tax-collectors; he even invited the rich to become his disciples. Liberation theology by contrast is divisive; it is strident in proclaiming damnation for the rich oppressors (the two words are a synonymous coupling), for whom there is no mercy. There are some things of which I am sure about Jesus, and one of them is that the proclamation of unforgiving hatred of one's fellow men and women is entirely foreign to all he said, all he stood for and all he was. This seems so obvious a component of any doctrine (or ideology) which claims to be Christian that it puzzles me when theologians do not notice its absence; and I am not thinking only of liberation theologians. It seems to me that we Christians (God forgive us) are willing to postpone reconciliation until we have our way. In this feature theologians show themselves no more unchristian than their adversaries of the Roman Curia, who must also have trouble saying the Lord's Prayer. This does not recommend liberation theology to me as a legitimate presentation of the gospel to the modern world.

My third reason for rejecting liberation theology is more subtle and, I am sure, more controversial. I put it more briefly than it deserves when I say that it is the candid hopes and plans that the reign of God will be brought to pass by political means. If anyone has followed me thus far, he or she will be able to recognize that by this I mean: if people will not do what we think is right, then by God we will make them do it. I have already given my reasons (perhaps not enough reasons, but that is all I have) for believing that this is foreign to the gospel. Just as Jesus left no directions nor example for the acquisition and use of wealth, so he left us no directions nor example for the acqusition and use of political power. The wedding of liberation theology to politics seems to be clearly recognized; it seems to be the reason why the Supreme Pontiff has effectively disowned it (not as effectively as he disowned Hans Küng). Perhaps the Supreme Pontiff and I are saying the same thing for different reasons. I feel fairly sure that my apolitical interpretation of the life and "teaching" of Jesus will no more please his Holiness than the politics of liberation theology. At this juncture, when I find myself likely to have made enemies of both parties, I have naught but the cold comfort of the reflection that I must be doing something right.

My fourth reason for rejecting liberation theology is its ambiguity about the use of violence as a political means. I say ambiguity because that is what I read; liberation theologians seem neither clearly to accept violence as an extension of politics nor clearly to reject it. As far as I can see, they have bought the ethics of the just war (or the just revolution); I hope I have made it clear that I am a convinced pacifist. It seems fair to say that we are talking about a theology of revolution. It seems clear that revolutions are and always have been the violent overthrow of existing political institutions. I suppose I should know that oppressors are not overthrown except by violent revolution. I suppose I should know too that oppressors maintain themselves only by institutionalized violence. I do know these things, possibly because I have read more history than most liberation theologians. I will stipulate that it is unfair to symbolize the Russian revolution of 1917 by the gunning down of a helpless family, most of them children, in the basement of a house. I will be glad to be told what is an apt symbol—perhaps the liquidation of the kulaks? I will stipulate further that it is unfair to the French revolutionaries of 1789 to say that their revolution is symbolized by the guillotine. It makes no difference; in both cases the oppressors had bloody hands, and the revolutionaries had bloody hands as well; there is your symbol—bloody hands. But you cannot make an omelet without breaking eggs, can you?

Why do we think that violence, like drinking, will be cured by a hair of the dog that bit us? It is a matter of established fact that in neither revolution mentioned was oppression removed nor the oppressed liberated; they

simply got a new set of oppressors. It takes very little skill
in speech or writing to say clearly that one rejects violence
whether it is committed by the oppressors or by the oppressed, and no theological education to see that Jesus
with the machine gun does not come off as an authentic
figure. I credit liberation theologians both with theological
education and with the skill to write what they mean, so I
must conclude that the ambiguity I mentioned is
deliberate. As Jesus left no directions on the acquisition
and use of power, so he left no directions on the use of
violence, even saving the due proportion between the good
end to be achieved and the damage which must be done to
achieve it. I said above that Jesus taught us much about
how to die; he taught and showed us nothing about how to
kill. The renunciation of violence can be dangerous; we are
subject to a barrage of propaganda that the use of violence
is less dangerous. Since the biblical myth of Eden has become weak in its symbolism for modern readers, might it
not be better for homiletic purposes to say that original sin
was the sin of Cain? It is not without interest that the
hominids discovered by Leakey in Africa from 1,800,000
B.C. had invented weapons which they used against their
own kind with fatal results. For cynics like me that answers
the question whether these creatures were human with an
unqualified affirmative. It is doubtful that they had yet invented the private ownership of property.

Let me conclude with a quotation from Hans Küng. I
quote it not because he agrees with me—he does not—but
because he writes with a characteristic moderation which I,
perhaps less wisely, have not chosen to imitate. But the
reader should know that my judgment in this matter is not
final, as it is in nothing I write. If it is not as clear as two

and two are four, why should I present it as if it were?

    ... theology will be understood as something more than an abstract theology of secularization, as "a theological reflection of the experience of shared efforts to abolish the current unjust situation and to build a different society, freer and more human," where "people can live with dignity and be the agents of their own destiny." A theology, that is, which is ethically oriented and wholly concentrated on practice; to be more exact, on "liberation praxis." It would be a theology turned in these countries against all brutal oppression, whether politico-social (the poor, downtrodden, weak), erotic-sexual (woman as sex object) or pedagogical (children educated in an oligarchic-repressive educational system). This theology would seek to present a historical project of political, economic, cultural, sexual liberation, as a true sign and anticipation of the definitive eschatological project of complete freedom in the kingdom of God.

    Not only theology, however, but also the Church—which so often in the centuries of colonial Christendom and right up to the present time betrayed its own program—may no longer misuse the Gospel of Jesus Christ to justify a social situation clearly contradicting the requirements of the Gospel. The Gospel may no longer be distorted and turned into an ideology, sanctioned by the Church, useful to a thin, excessively wealthy upper stratum for satisfying the religious needs of the masses and so securing a social order which is set up and dominated only by a few and is of service and advantage only to a few. The Church, for which the claim to universal liberation in Christ cannot be restricted solely to the religious plane, must identify itself differently from what it has done hitherto with the wretched condition of large masses of the people, with their hopes and struggles for a better human existence. And so the fact cannot be overlooked that Christians—from workers up to priests and bishops—are getting involved to an increasing extent in the liberation process: "liberation *from* an overall system of oppression and liberation *for* the self-realization of the people, enabling them to determine for themselves their political, economic and cultural destiny."

"Commitment for liberation" then along the whole line! But here we must be cautious about slogans. For this oppression and a number of things said and demanded in this context are *vague and ambiguous.* "Even today in Latin America it can be utilized for ideological or party political ends." Cannot "theology of liberation" easily become a mere shell of a word, filled with the most violently contrasted political contents: from the opinions of relatively conservative theologians to the explicitly Marxist arguments of revolutionaries? Most leading advocates of a "theology of liberation" of course see that great danger: that the Christian message, which cannot be identified with any existing or future social order, might be reduced to a political program or a political campaign. It is fully recognized that the participation of Christians in the liberation process "varies in radicalism," using tentative expressions in "a process of searching and advancing by 'trial and error.' " Those involved would like to keep "several options" open, not only for directly political, but also educational, cultural, economic, pastoral-prophetic activity. The main interest of this theology is not socio-political or economic to satisfy party selfishness. Here too man should not live by bread alone, although many would be glad if they were able to do just this. There is an intense search for a new synthesis of the "militant-committed" and the "religious-contemplative" factors, of action and prayer, mysticism and politics, and an attempt to bring this to life. And the living testimony of poverty in particular—as expression of love of neighbor and testimony against injustice, not as an ideal of life valuable in itself or as glorifying the inhuman reality—acquires a special significance in the specific social conditions of the poor countries.

In practice, for Latin-American Christians, the discussion on the political-social realization of the impulse to liberation centers on the question: does not the commitment to liberation necessarily mean a political option for *socialism* against *capitalism?* The widespread sympathy for socialism particularly among active Christians is often the only way out of the outrageous conditions set up in this continent as a result of the capitalist economic system (but also of other factors often overlooked like climate, cultural historical development, prevailing mentality, attitude to life and work, established religion) and which are comparable only with those caused in the last century in Europe by the exploitation of Manchester Liberalism.[1]

I have written at some length—not as much as the topic justifies—about liberation theology because it is the most significant example of Christian scholars pledging their talents and their skills to political and social purposes. I wrote at length also because I have felt the allure of a movement which at least pretended—I am not questioning the integrity of any liberation theologians—to free theology from its historic role of intellectual lackey to the ruling propertied classes. I believe its proponents think that it does, and that this is the basic liberation which the movement promotes. I have given reasons why I think that it fails to achieve this liberation and why it exchanges one servitude for another. I regret this; and I see no reason why liberation theology should not in the future develop some genuine freedom for itself and become what it once promised to be, the first really new and original theological development in five hundred years. It may take no longer than it took theology to move from Abelard to Thomas Aquinas. If it does, I am afraid that I shall have gone to my reward (or something else), and I shall not be here to enjoy and share what I am sure will be an exhilarating and inspiring experience.

Following my established scheme, we shall now set forth the sayings of Jesus on the "intellectual life," which I admit are few, obscure and easily twisted by me as well as by others, in contrast with this sketch of worldly wisdom which, biased as it may be, is at least written by an insider.

VII. SALVATION THROUGH FOLLY

God's folly is wiser than men,
And his weakness more powerful
than men.

—1 Corinthians 1:25

JESUS was not a learned man, and still less was he a professional scholar. The Gospels relate that he was given the title of "rabbi," which means "my teacher," but at that time academic titles were not earned and accredited like modern degrees. The title (which a Jewish friend, now deceased, assured me is not found in Jewish literature of the first century) could be applied to anyone who seemed to deserve some special respect. I have often been called "doctor" by complete strangers, usually because the titles "father" or "reverend" stuck in their throats. The remark quoted in John 7:15 denying that Jesus had the education acquired from elder scribes is supported by the gibes attributed to his Nazarene neighbors in Mark 6:2 and Matthew 13:54. Even in the first century of our era academics (and non-academics) had begun to look for proper academic credentials, which Jesus lacked entirely. What can be made out of the fact that he could easily have acquired them I do not know. The scribes instructed students gratuitously and were rather proud of it (unlike their modern successors), and if Jesus could have found the leisure to become an itinerant preacher he could certainly have found the leisure to sit at the feet of some scribe.

Jesus was not only not a professional scholar, his relations with the learned establishment of his time and place seem to have been uniformly hostile. The degree of hostil-

ity which existed between Jesus and the scribes is a matter
of dispute; my own opinion is colored by my conviction
that Jesus never closed the door in the face of anyone. This
does not mean that he accepted what anyone said or did
without saying that he thought it was wrong when it
deserved such criticism. One may accept the conclusions of
my colleagues (one can hardly do anything else here) that
the clear hostility exhibited towards scribes in the Gospels
has been colored by the hostility between primitive Christians and Jews who thought their Christian fellow Jews
were renegades and thus is not an entirely faithful tradition
of what Jesus said about the scribes. Any discussion based
upon the Gospel texts concerning this topic must proceed
with the utmost caution. This does not mean it may not
proceed at all. With all due reservations made, it seems
safe to say that if the relations between Jesus and the
scribes were warm and cordial, the Gospels have so
distorted them that we can honestly doubt whether we can
trust them as sources about anything. I suppose some
would accept this conclusion and say that we know nothing
about Jesus, so why discuss his attitude about anything? I
have already dealt with this problem; I mention it again because it emerges again with unusual sharpness.

Jesus exhibited no response to Gentile learning, which in
his world meant Greek learning. It is, I believe, safe to say
that Palestinian Jews had rejected Greek learning as folly
on the simple grounds that the Greeks were idolaters and
therefore fools and could teach believers in the one true
God nothing. The Palestinian Jews did not seem to have
shared the curiosity of many Alexandrian Jews which led
them to dabble with Greek learning. That Jesus shared this
hostility does not appear in the Gospels; all that appears is
total nescience of Greek learning. In spite of many forms

of popular orthodox belief about Jesus, he really was and did not merely pretend to be a Palestinian villager. The Incarnation was not a slumming tour by a heavenly aristocrat. The only learning which the Palestinian scribes thought deserved the name of wisdom was the knowledge of the Scriptures, especially the five books of the Torah, and in addition a growing body of scribal commentary on the Torah, preserved in oral tradition and not collected in writing until 200 A.D. Modern people do not realize the feats of memory performed in ancient times by bright people who were illiterate, as most of the population were. My point is that the only learning and the only learned men to whom Jesus had any attitude were the written word of God and the scribes who interpreted it.

Bearing in mind the reservations made above about the use of the Gospel text, it must be said that the sayings of Jesus exhibit the minimum of respect and esteem towards the professional scholars of his world. Perhaps the most laudatory remark preserved is Matthew 23:2: the scribes and Pharisees sit in the chair of Moses. Therefore do as they tell you, but not as they do. This is certainly a left-handed compliment. It reminds me of the well worn faculty joke: those who can, do; those who cannot do, teach (and those who cannot teach go into administration). The remark quoted in Mark 12:34 is more simply complimentary to a single scribe; the scribe praises the answer of Jesus to the question of the greatest commandment, and in turn is told that he is not far from the reign of God. This passage illustrates the way in which the anti-scribe bias of the Gospels is developed. Matthew omits the compliment to the scribe (22:34-40). Luke (10:25-36) also omits the compliment, but replaces it with another question which elicits the parable of the Good Samaritan, which the scribe accepts grudgingly, and thus appears less favorably even than in Matthew. There can hardly be any doubt that if the words of Jesus are preserved here at all, they are best preserved in Mark; and I am not questioning the authenticity of the parable of the Good Samaritan. The reference to the scribe learned in the reign of God (Matthew 13:52), unparalleled in the other Gospels, is not a reference to Jewish scribes, but to Christian scribes of the primitive Christian communities. That such remarks are preserved at all suggests that Jesus was not totally hostile to the scribes, and that they were "redactionally" modified suggests their authenticity. Their number suggests that not many were known or remembered, and one may venture the assertion that Jesus had better relations with tax-collectors and prostitutes or even with the wealthy than he did with scholars, to call them by a modern cultural term.

It must be recognized that the invective against the scribes (and the Pharisees) preserved in Matthew 23 was not delivered by Jesus at one blast, and that Matthew never intended to say that it was. It is true that Matthew has with some sense of dramatic tension placed it at the end of the story of the relations between Jesus and the scribes. This does not entitle us to say that these relations reached their climax in such a confrontation; life (you may take this from one who has lived most of his quota of actuarial expectations) is rarely dramatic. Our question now is not when Jesus said these things or how many of these things he said but whether Jesus ever said any of these things: whether they are not entirely the composition of the evangelists and their sources, intended to reflect a hostility which many of us (if not most) are sure existed without an equal assurance that it was thus expressed. The invective against the scribes in Matthew is like the Sermon on the

Mount; it collects in one discourse sayings most of which are found in the other Gospels in different contexts, many of which are accepted as authentic sayings of Jesus. To treat the invective as something different from the Sermon on the Mount and to criticize and interpret it by different methods seem to me, if you pardon my rudeness, to introduce some quite unbiblical notions into exegesis. I know we all do this; so it becomes a question of the validity of the assumptions. The assumption here is that a group of Jews were all governed by what is now called anti-Semitism. As this assumption cannot be demonstrated, so with a convinced believer it cannot be refuted, and I shall not attempt to refute it.

Therefore I shall simply recapitulate briefly the heads under which the criticisms of the scribes attributed to Jesus can be grouped, with no attempt to say how often he said these things or how much the texts retain of the tone in which he said them. We shall ask whether these heads represent in any instance things which it appears Jesus could not have said—in a word, whether they are credible reports of his sayings. The list is rather long even in summary. Jesus charges the scribes with not practicing what they preach, with undue severity and rigorism in interpreting obligations, with a love of display and of tokens and titles of honor, with withholding the truth, with concentration on the trivial to the neglect of what is really important, with concern for appearances and lack of concern for the reality which lies beneath appearances, with veneration of the past and no effort to learn from the past. These details lie at the base of the general charge of "hypocrisy." There are other charges elsewhere in the Gospels (like devouring the houses of widows while they recite long prayers, Mark 12:40), but my interest here is not to collect all the anti-scribal remarks found in the Gospels; I simply inquire whether these remarks are basically faithful to what was remembered of Jesus. The invective of Matthew is responsible for the meaning of "pharisaic" in the English dictionary, which sticks like a burr to the hide of Jews as the adjective "jesuitical" sticks to the hide of Jesuits—and, I suppose, as "puritanical" sticks to members of old New England families or "dutch courage" to members of some old New York families.

I said our first task is to see whether these remarks contain anything which Jesus could not have said, and I think we owe this discussion, shallow as it may be, both to the scribes and to Jesus. The Gospels present a picture of scribes as a body (admitting individual exceptions) who rejected Jesus and whatever it was that he proclaimed. I know nothing in the attitude of scribes at the time or scribes since which would compel me to think that as a body they could ever have been sympathetic to anyone who showed the attitude towards the Law and Jewish observances which Jesus is reported to have shown. In the language of the scribes Jesus was an *am-haarets,* an ignorant and ill-mannered clod. This is so obvious that there has never been a lack of scholars in modern times to say that the attitude ascribed to Jesus by the Gospels was not the attitude of Jesus but of primitive Christians. This leads, as I have pointed out, to the further question of whether the hostility between Jesus and the scribes was not created from whole cloth by the evangelists and their sources. It has occurred to me, as I think about this problem, that it is possible that primitive Christians found a hostility which they did not create; this possibility seems quite real, and this explains their writings as well as unproved theory that a group of Jews turned anti-Jewish.

I am sorry to be taking so long to get to the point, which, I remind both my readers and myself, is the credibility of the attribution of these remarks to Jesus—in substance, I repeat, and not in verbal formulation. Actually once I get to the point, I will be surprisingly brief. Here I suppose one must first ask whether the remarks are credible in themselves. Are they defamatory? If they are, I will lose interest in Jesus and the Gospels rather quickly. There is a sense in which all remarks about a group or a class are defamatory. This does not keep such general remarks out of the common language—it does not keep them out now (even of the language of liberal people), it did not in ancient times, and it did not keep them out of the Bible. I have done some reading in collections from Talmudic sources (like most Gentiles I am out of my depth in the Talmud), and I am assured that no criticism of the scribes is attributed to Jesus which was not uttered by the scribes themselves about each other. These remarks show as little originality as anything in the Gospels. If Jesus said things like this, it was not for them that the scribes were hostile. They were hostile because he was perceived to be attacking the very foundations of Judaism. I said above that I believe that Jesus never slammed the door in the face of anyone. The same breadth has not always been shown by his disciples, even by those who took up the task of recording the words attributed to him. I have noticed elsewhere places where Jesus was too big to be grasped by his disciples, ancient and modern.

There are a few other passages of the Gospels which bear somewhat indirectly upon the topic of learning; and if anyone thinks I am dragging them in by the hair of the head, there is not much I can say except that when people think they are being attacked the instinctive response is defensive. Let me remove any uncertainty from the minds of my colleagues; they are being attacked. The first of these sayings is the one called the meteor from the Johannine heavens fallen into the Synoptic Gospels (more precisely, into Q; Matthew 11:25; Luke 10:21). I am not calling into attention the following verses in Matthew and Luke, the lines which have a "Johannine" ring, but to these verses alone, which to my knowledge have nothing Johannine about them, whatever that may be thought to mean. In this line (verbally identical in the two Gospels) Jesus thanks his father that he has concealed these things from the *sophoi* (wise) and *synetoi* (clever, understanding) and revealed them to the *nepioi* (simple; when applied to adults, simpletons). What are "these things"? They can hardly be anything else but the proclamation of the reign of God; one hesitates to say that "these things" are the "doctrine" of Jesus. I said earlier that Jesus does not really appear as a "teacher" proposing "doctrine"; if these or similar terms must be used, he is better called a guide or a leader who shows a way. This line certainly uses words which suggest teachers, students and learning; I do not think I am wrong when I suggest that these terms are used derisively. It is from those who deal with learning professionally that Jesus says that God has concealed the "way" which he shows; by using the crutch of biblical circumlocution we understand this to mean not that God is responsible for their failure to understand, but that they have refused to learn. In no case is the "doctrine" of any teacher ever within the reach of simpletons.

There may be no saying of Jesus which is more deeply critical of professional learned men than this text. It was on the basis of this line that I wrote some years ago that what Jesus said was within the grasp of anyone who had reached the mental age of twelve. The simple see at once that the "way" of Jesus is very hard to do, but easy to understand. It takes real cleverness and sophisticated intelligence to find ways to evade and distort the clear meaning of what Jesus said and to find reasons why his words are not applicable to a more advanced and more sophisticated culture which he never shared and to which he never spoke. It takes a university education to see that 2000 years of progress have produced a world too complex for the simplistic approach of Jesus to the problems of life in society. Perhaps we need no more than some complications of syntax to paraphrase the saying; Jesus is so simplistic that he makes things difficult, but let me try: "I am glad, Father, that although the smart and the learned people, the best and the brightest, find what I say too simple for them to think it deserves their attention, there are simpletons to whom I can talk and be understood."

Do I sound like an anti-intellectual? Let me repeat (it may be tedious by this time) that I have been a professional smart-aleck for 50 years. I said above that I think I have encountered more than my share of anti-intellectuals, although what a fair share of them is may be disputed. I want to say that while smart-alecks are often intolerable, dumb smart-alecks, to coin an oxymoron, are always intolerable and worse than that; they are dangerous. People who say that the study of the Bible and other theological material is unimportant for the true believer are worse than arrogant (which they are), worse than people who say they do not need road maps (concealing the fact that they cannot read them), worse than people who never read directions (admitting that the prose of written directions is usually more dense than Kant). Your smart-aleck who poses as a true believer loves to believe things which are not so, and refuses to see or to admit that for faith it makes a difference. I mentioned above that I was warned early in life about the pride which is the occupational vice of the smart student and the intellectual. Our instructors seemed to think that the ignorant needed no warning against pride. The pride of the smart-aleck is more easily borne than the pride of a dumb ignoramus. Hence I think that if I am burning what I once adored by writing in these terms, I know at least what I am burning; the anti-intellectual does not know.

I trust that after this declaration no one will think that I mean any sympathy for the anti-intellectual when I turn to the next and perhaps the most difficult saying of Jesus concerning this topic. It is so difficult—at least I find it so—that I could not quarrel with anyone who said that it is not authentic, it is an invention of some primitive scribe who understood the meaning of Jesus about as well as Luke understood the construction of a Palestinian dirt roof (Luke 5:19). But this is the easy way out of a difficulty, and we smart-alecks despise cheap solutions. The saying is found in Mark 10:13-16; Matthew 18:1-4; Luke 18:15-17. It is found in a simple story of Jesus allowing himself to be touched by small children in spite of the scolding of the disciples. He not only accepted the children, he said: "Let them alone; it is just to such as these that the reign of God belongs. If you cannot accept the reign of God like a child, you do not belong in it." Matthew, unlike Mark and Luke, associates this saying with a dispute about greatness. This element, which may be foreign to the original form of the saying, is certainly not foreign to the sayings of Jesus; whether it belongs here or not is not, I believe, important to my purpose. It is startling that Jesus is credited with a saying which not only expresses less than due respect for wisdom and learning, as the saying just previously quoted does, but which states flatly that even mature intelligence is an obstacle to sharing in the reign of God. This is a more intolerable paradox than saying that wealth is an obstacle to sharing in the reign of God. This specifies the saying of Jesus that his follower must deny his very self, say that he does not exist (Mark 8:34; Matthew 16:24; Luke 9:23). Jesus meant more by the denial of self than fasting and the wearing of sack-cloth, certainly more than temporary abstinence from whisky, tobacco and moving pictures.

What could he have meant by saying that you must put off your mature intelligence? Since I refuse to hide behind such dodges as "Semitic exaggeration" (who ever proved that the speakers of Semitic languages exaggerate more than the speakers of Indo-European languages?), I am forced to ask whether my adult intelligence and experience have not, like the simple anti-intellectual faith of the true believer, left me convinced with no necessity for critical self-examination of a great many things that are not true. In short, maybe Jesus meant that there are problems in my life and in human life which are met (not necessarily solved) not by knowledge, reasoning and a disciplined in-tellect, but only by love as simple and trusting as the love of a child, by forgiveness (the children call it "making up"), by preferring, like some of my very young friends, only those games in which everyone is a winner. In my case, I am now too old to dash it off by saying "He could not have meant what it seems to mean" and leave it as one of the great unsolved riddles of the Gospels. Why, it would upset my whole scheme of values to which I have dedicated all my adult life, a little more than 50 years. And I am hardly a richer man because I have long ago destroyed my

capacity to love and forgive and yield as a child can love
and forgive and yield. The intellectual is competitive. In a
society which teaches its young to be competitive, the intellectual is the teacher and the model of what he teaches
his students to become.

But let us get back to the brass tacks of the text. Jesus
was not talking about modern learned and professional
persons, about those who have dedicated their lives and
their talents to the cultivation of skills on which the fabric
of modern civilization survives, skills of which Jesus was
completely unaware and with which he never dealt. Does
this mean that we have developed a wisdom which is completely beyond his? How committed are we to the intellect?
If our commitment is so total that we cannot deny it and
ourselves, let us intellectuals assert ourselves and say that
we have no problems for which Jesus said or did anything
to help us. Let theologians and biblicists continue to play
their games of scrabble, blind man's bluff, pin the tail on
the donkey, and "button, button, who's got the button?",
content that they are not expected to say anything pertinent to the human condition in which they live. In fact, the
less pertinent they remain, the more likely they are to be
supported by those who do not know what they are doing,
but know vaguely that high culture is supposed to support
that sort of thing. They will touch men's minds and business about as much as the opera and the ballet do, but they
will not be as much fun to watch. The world has just gone
too far beyond Jesus; it has become what so many have
hoped for, post-Christian. I am still enough of a theist
(whatever that may mean) to wonder whether the world
will have the last word on that; this I must touch upon in
my final chapters.

Granted that Jesus spoke in and to a different world, I

wonder whether those who think the story of his words and deeds is important enough to justify a department in the graduate school of modern universities do not owe it to the object of their studies as scribes to give themselves a test formed on the text of Matthew 23, omitting those features of the text which have been rendered antiquated by the progress of modern scholarship. I have done this for myself, and I found no features I could omit; but I have grown old and my scholarship shows signs of senescence. I will not tell you what evalaution I reached; but the test was more revealing than I liked.

TEMPTATION III: IN THE CEMETERY

AGAIN we are in the valley which lies between the Temple mountain and the Mount of Olives, in a cemetery not far from the olive grove of Gethsemane. A full day has elapsed since the encounter of Yeshu and Nick in the olive grove. In the depths of the valley of the Kidron one can barely perceive that the first light of day has appeared. Yeshu is alone. He is seated on an enormous circular stone; in the dim light it takes a closer look to see that the stone is cut to cover the aperture at the opening of a large tomb, in front of which it lies. Yeshu shows the evident marks of brutal physical violence. His expression shows great inner peace and serenity, the expression of one who has just accomplished a very difficult task. Yet it is the expression of one slightly dazed, the countenance of one who has just escaped something threatening and does not quite believe it.

A figure suddenly appears in the dim light, striding rapidly towards Yeshu. It is Nick, less jaunty than usual; in fact, he seems to have lost his customary aplomb. He looks like a man who has just missed a train, frustrated and angry. He strides up to Yeshu and glares at him, but Yeshu anticipates his speech:

YESHU: Good morning, Nick. I am surprised to see you up so early. Did you have a pleasant Passover?

NICK: Where in hell have you been?

YESHU: About the ninth circle, I think; I did not pay much attention to the scenery. If you get to the first circle you are surely dead.

NICK: No wise cracks, please; this is too important. How did you pull it off? I know you died; I saw that centurion ram his lance in nearly up to his elbow. So what is the trick?

YESHU: Shall I say that we have a few techniques that we are not quite ready to go public with?

NICK: Oh, an irrepressible wit; but I cannot blame you for a bit of gloating. Gloating should be beneath you, Yeshu.

YESHU: I am not gloating, Nick. I died as surely as our father Abraham (to whom I spoke just yesterday), and Adonai raised me up to life. It is as simple as that, and you do not believe it.

NICK: Neither will anyone else. Adonai has never done a thing like this before.

YESHU: I suppose you know him so well that you think he can never surprise you?

NICK: Suppose he did; Yeshu, we have to make a deal.

YESHU: Nick, every time we meet you always come up with a deal. For the third and last time, no deal. I am not doing anything to help you do anything. You should know by this time that I do not need you, and that you cannot hurt me.

NICK: And I do not need you, and you cannot hurt me.

YESHU: Are you sure?

NICK: Yes, because I have outlived everybody, and I will outlive you. But while I still do not know what you are after, there is no reason why we cannot make a deal.

YESHU: What do you have in mind?

NICK: You cannot make anything, even out of rising from the dead, without my help. I have all the talent—the orators, the poets, the writers, the artists, the men with power, the men with money. Whatever it is that you are promoting—and there must be something—you cannot do it without the resources I control. You cannot do anything with those clods you picked up, your "disciples"—ha! They could not learn the alphabet or count beyond ten without taking off both sandals. They ran and hid the day before yesterday, and they have not been found yet. Are you thinking of matching these peasants with the political, financial and intellectual establishment of the Roman world?

YESHU: With all that, why do you need me?

NICK: Because I cannot allow a man who rises from the dead to run around loose. He can cause all sorts of trouble to my plans unless he is controlled. Frankly, Yeshu, I am not sure I can control you, and I do not trust you to support me.

YESHU: All right, I have a counter-proposition.

NICK: I knew that you would see reason. Together, Yeshu, we can subdue the world with much less time and trouble than I had expected. State your proposition.

YESHU: Die.

NICK: Are you out of your mind? I am Anthropos (the Son of Man to you barbarians) and I am immortal, I cannot die.

YESHU: Oh yes you can, Nick; do it and see whether Adonai will raise you. Then we can deal with each other on equal terms.

NICK: I suppose that is what you meant when you talked that nonsense about dying to yourself and taking up your cross?

YESHU: I meant death for you; and it is going to happen to you, Nick, whether you accept it or not.

NICK: That is inconceivable.

YESHU: As inconceivable as a man rising from the dead?

NICK: I am sorry we cannot make a deal; and it looks as if we cannot part friends.

YESHU: That is right, Nick. Maybe you are beginning to understand me.

NICK: I am less disappointed because I could not
           recruit you.

YESHU: Why is that, Nick?

NICK: Only a few days ago a young Jew came to
           Jerusalem from Tarsus. His name is Saul, and
           he wants to study to become a scribe. Smart as
           a whip! He is almost as smart as you, Yeshu,
           and that is saying a lot; I never doubted your
           talent. I shall replace you with him as a can-
           didate for a high position in my enterprises.
           And I may add that although he knows nothing
           about you except hearsay, he is already con-
           vinced that Yeshu was an impostor. He would
           not believe in you if you walked up to him and
           knocked him over. I shall handle this promising
           young recruit very carefully; I do not want
           another fiasco like the one with you.

YESHU: I am sorry I cannot wish you luck, Nick; but I
           suppose you never run out of apt candidates to
           do your work.

NICK: That is exactly right, Yeshu; and that is why it
           is foolish for you to match yourself against me.

While Nick is still speaking, he is startled to realize that
Yeshu is not listening; he is no longer there. Without a
sound or a movement he has disappeared from the stone
where he was sitting. Nick is not only startled, he is
alarmed. He speaks:

NICK: Yeshu! Yeshu!
           Where are you?
           Is someone pulling my leg?

VIII. THIS IS THE WAY
THE WORLD ENDS

Tell us, when will this occur?
What will be the sign
that all this is coming to an end?

—Mark 13:4

WITH what degree of persuasiveness I do not know, I have tried to set up the essential opposition between the cultural pillars of western civilization and the will of God as we Christians believe that will was revealed by Jesus Christ. Almost every step of this exposition has been disputable. I do not pretend to have dealt with all the points under dispute, nor to have adduced all the evidence which can be adduced in favor of my theses or which tells against them. Those who recognize disputed points which have been omitted from discussion or important evidence which is relevant in favor of my positions or against them may conclude that I did not think they were important enough to warrant dispute or have been subsumed implicitly under other heads of the discussion, or that I am ignorant of these points. I am not presenting a history of western thought on the scale of the Durants' *Story of Civilization* or Arnold Toynbee's *A Study of History*. If the job were to be done on that scale it would certainly take as long as these two works did. And since I did not conceive the idea until I had reached an age at which I cannot reasonably count on that number of years, it will be understood why I am doing something much more lightweight.

But since my concern has been the essential opposition between God (for that it is really what I mean) and western

216

civilization, let me say that the opposition is not only essential, it is lethal; I mean that western civilization will kill God if it can or, since I believe that God is indestructible, it will kill itself trying. Do I leave the question there, or ask whether Jesus spoke to that question? It does not seem too much to say that western civilization has reached a point where it believes that it does not need God; it is totally Epicurean. It is not yet prevailingly atheistic; most of the western world finds the militant atheism of Marxism offensive. I see nothing in the ideology of most of the western world to keep it from adopting militant atheism. I have no idea how many people, even in the United States where I have spent my life, think that religion is a factor of importance in the decisions, individual and collective, which govern their daily lives. Unless I have totally misunderstood the public ethos and the fundamental beliefs of Christianity, the number of people who believe that Christianity is of any importance in deciding how to live cannot be large.

I suppose I could ask my readers to ask themselves (as I have asked myself) in how many decisions in the course of a day does religious motivation play any significant part. And if the reader is a professional religious person (as I am) or if they think themselves as religious as the average, or at least not notoriously irreligious, the conclusion about the place of religion in American life may be appalling. It is something like asking how many decisions in the course of a day have already been made for me by someone else; it gives one a more realistic view of one's personal freedom.

If this signifies the importance and value of religion in American life, how much would it take to turn public opinion to militant atheism? I am not talking about persecution, although it would be stupid to deny the possibility. I just do not think that we religious people have ever been, or in my lifetime are likely to become, so annoying to the dominant ethos of western civilization that we will deserve persecution. Accommodation is a game which we Christians play very well. But I am talking about public support and public sympathy of the kind which has enabled the churches to do whatever it is that they do. I am talking about a return of the church to the catacombs, again not in the sense of persecution, but in the sense of dropping out of sight, of the loss of any influence whatever on public life and on the private lives of anyone except the few survivors of their shrunken membership.

Nor am I talking about other countries than the country in which I have spent my life and in which I expect to die. Of other countries and continents I cannot speak from personal knowledge and experience. What I see as possible in the United States seems possible in other countries which share the same culture with the United States. I believe that both here and elsewhere the church can avoid persecution or going into the catacombs by surviving as it has so far, that is, by being the lackey of the establishment of wealth and power; that is, by not being the church. Whether one thinks this is the way it will survive depends on what one believes about the indefectibility of the church. I may state my personal belief, with no claim to impose it on others, that this is not the way the church will survive; I believe that would be the ultimate failure and death of the church. Therefore the church will ultimately refuse to surrender and even to compromise and so by dying to the world it will find its life. But to many it will appear to be death. With some insight Daniel A. Lord, S. J., wrote in a piece of fiction he composed in the late 1930s (a nervous period) words which he put in the mouth of his fictitious totalitarian villain: Jesus promised his church indefectibility, but he did not promise it indefectibility in the United States—and I am going to destroy it here.

Prophecy is cheap and easy; the prophet, if he projects a sufficiently distant future, is quite safe from the obligation of explaining his failure to predict it with anything near accuracy. Some hesitant guesses about the way the future might go which I have sketchily attempted and will set forth in the following chapter are not only uncertain, but they still do not answer the question: is the opposition between God and western civilization to continue indefinitely? And if it does, must we not consider humankind, or at least the vast majority of humankind—if we are correct in thinking that the domination of western civilization over the world will continue and grow—as a failure of God to achieve his purpose? Must we not consider that God has produced an anti-God which he cannot control? Must we not renounce any form of belief which has yet been expressed and restate our creed: I believe in Man the being almighty, the lord and the maker of a new heavens and a new earth? Have we reached or are we very near the point where we do not need God, where he can neither help us nor hurt us? What rewards does he apportion, what punishments does he inflict? Are not his "laws" the manufacture of an atavistic sense of guilt called conscience? What meaning and validity can be imputed to his alleged "judgments," all of which are quite explicable facts of history and the natural sciences without any reference to any supposed transcendental reality? It is not so much that God is non-existent as that he/she has become irrelevant.

Since I do believe in the reality of God (because it is patent nonsense to say that humankind or "nature" is the supreme being), I am compelled to believe that a continuing anti-God is a contradiction in terms. To answer my own question, the conflict cannot endure; there must be a resolution. And since a belief in God is a belief in his supremacy, the resolution must be dictated on his terms. And since God has created humankind a race of free intelligent beings, I believe the resolution must respect human freedom and intelligence. And since this resolution is obviously beyond the capacity of humankind in its known historical reality, I am again driven back to the reality of God, because no one else can do it. So far I have advanced by my wits—leaning, of course, on the collected wisdom of several thousand years. Now I can turn to the question whether Jesus was credited with saying anything to the question which I have raised.

The answer at first seems obvious. What is called "the synoptic apocalypse" is found in Mark 13:1-37; Matthew 24:1-51; Luke 21:5-36. With remarkably fewer variations than appear, for instance, in the sayings collected in Matthew's Sermon on the Mount, or in the parable discourses of all three Gospels, the synoptics report a discourse in which Jesus announces both the impending destruction of Jerusalem (which occurred in 70 A.D., about 40 years after the death of Jesus) and the physical destruction of the external world, followed by the appearance of the "Son of Man" before the entire human race. Hardly any interpreter doubts that Jesus himself is meant here by the Son of Man. There are clear mythological traits in the manifestation of the Son of Man, and one may wonder, as I do, whether the "Second Coming" is other than a mythological image (not necessarily due to Jesus) of something which is not clear to us interpreters.

The cosmic collapse which is called "the end of the world" is not dissimilar from cosmic collapses found in other mythologies; the biblical deluge, borrowed from ancient Mesopotamia, is an example of a cosmic collapse and restoration. The Stoics thought the world would perish in fire after 10,000 years and be reborn after the catastrophe. Wagner has made thousands of viewers familiar with the Norse *Ragnarok,* the twilight of the gods, in which even Valhalla, the palace of the gods, would fall in flames, and the whole world would sleep eternally in the deep freeze of ice—a peculiarly Nordic way of thinking of it, one must say. Modern astronomy has acquainted the popular mind with the idea of "worlds in collision," to borrow the title of a very stupid book on the Bible published over 30 years ago. The theory which identifies cosmosgenesis with a "big bang" has somewhat acquainted the popular mind with the big bang which will wipe us out—and nobody in the cosmos will notice that anything has happened. And the possibility of a man-made world catastrophe of uncertain dimensions through the abuse of thermonuclear energy has been thrust into our consciousness.

In the world in which Jesus lived the idea of the end of the world and indeed of its proximity was current, if the books collected under the heading of apocalyptic literature are any guide to current popular belief of the first century. I have never been sure that they are. But these books, almost all of Jewish origin, attest to a variety of beliefs in an impending catastrophic end of the world which only the righteous or God's chosen people will survive. Besides the "Synoptic apocalypse," the only New Testament example of such books is the Revelation of John, but there are brief allusions in a few other books (for example, 2 Peter, Jude). Thus it would seem that there is no reason why any sayings attributed to Jesus about the catastrophic end of the world should be foreign to the world of Jewish belief in which he spoke. It was much less strange than his sayings about renouncing wealth and violence or forgiving one's enemies. The Synoptic apocalypse seems to have as much claim to be taken seriously as preserving the substance of what Jesus said as other sayings which I have taken very seriously in the preceding pages.

And that is just my problem—it is too much at home in popular speech and language, it seems to lack the radical novelty which we attribute to the gospel. Many interpreters view the Synoptic apocalypse as doubtfully authentic, and their reasons deserve consideration. My own judgment, which will emerge in the course of the discussion, is close enough to this opinion and sufficiently far from what some of my colleagues will call my "fundamentalist" approach to the sayings of Jesus to demand some comment, out of self-defense if nothing else. I beg to be forgiven for quoting an earlier writing of my own which still expresses my view:

> . . . —however much one can and ought to feel sympathy for the oppressed, their voice, when they can get away with it, is usually the voice of vindictive hatred. The apocalyptic judgment is a dream of how the oppressed become the oppressors.[1]

This may be a conviction formed on *a priori* grounds, but I cannot identify Jesus with anything written or spoken in these tones, and I believe any saying attributed to him, authentic or not, is totally in opposition to these tones. Therefore I cannot believe that Jesus borrowed anything from the apocalyptic which would indicate that he accepted any piece of its ideology. I stick to my judgment in spite of the fact that the elements which I find offensive do not appear in the Synoptic apocalypse.

The renowned Albert Schweitzer created something of a

sensation when he resigned his post as professor of New Testament at Strasbourg (then in Germany) in 1905, became a doctor of medicine, and went to Africa to found and preside over a hospital, where he died in 1965. Schweitzer was one of the leading theologians who interpreted Jesus in the light of the Synoptic apocalypse; he believed that Jesus was convinced of the imminent end of the world and proclaimed it. Most interpreters have not been able to believe that one who fell into such a colossal error could be of any lasting religious significance. Schweitzer certainly had no problem in finding significance in the other sayings of Jesus; he renounced wealth and academic distinction and devoted himself to the service of the needy far more than I have done. I have mentioned the legend that in his later years he was rather difficult to deal with; this is not hard to understand. He had to rebuild his hospital after his fellow Christians destroyed it in the first World War. In spite of this weighty testimonial from one who showed more than a shallow understanding of the "way" of Jesus, I believe he was wrong in thinking that Jesus really believed in something so patently untrue as the imminent end of the world. But what did Jesus say about the end of the world? Schweitzer had to reject as the explanation of Christian scribes some clear denials that the end was imminent attributed to Jesus. His rejection is supported by the fairly clear belief of Paul in some of his letters that the time is short. One can say that the New Testament itself is ambiguous on the "imminence" of the end. I see no reason to put Jesus on one side or the other of this ambiguity.

The Synoptic apocalypse draws a clear distinction between the destruction of Jerusalem and the end-catastrophe. We can be fairly certain that this distinction does not go back to the original sayings of Jesus. When the Synoptic Gospels were written (and most interpreters would include Mark here, although a date before 70 A.D. can be argued for Mark), the destruction of Jerusalem was a fact of recent memory; the end catastrophe had not occurred (it has not yet occurred). The discourse attributes the distinction between the two events to Jesus himself. Where so much editorial work was obviously necessary the interpreter may well despair of ever recovering anything like the words of Jesus himself.

The announcement of the fall of Jerusalem certainly reflects accounts of the event told by witnesses. To such accounts should probably be attributed Luke's reference to the Roman siege practice of *circumvallatio*—digging a trench and building a wall around the entire besieged city. It is possible that Luke had done more reading in Roman manuals of warfare than he did in manuals of Palestinian house building, but I doubt it. If Jesus had announced the impending destruction of the Temple (which would have meant the destruction of the whole city), he would not have done more than Jeremiah did (Jeremiah 7:8-14). There is no doubt that such an announcement would have been received as the announcement of Jeremiah was (Jeremiah 26:1-19). Two of the Gospels do report that the charge of announcing the destruction of the Temple was laid against Jesus (Mark 14:58; Matthew 26:61), but this does not imply that the saying of Jesus occurred in an apocalyptic discourse. We have no idea how the same announcement made by Micah was received (Micah 3:12). That Jesus would not have been the first to announce this does not recommend the authenticity of the saying. The two events may have been hopelessly commingled in the announcement of a future catastrophe; but this would be mere speculation (the impatient reader may ask what I am doing now). If so, then any effort to find out what Jesus said seems doomed to fail. And if we do not understand his mind on this point, is it important? Schweitzer's example suggests that it is not.

I seem, then, to have pointed myself towards a suggestion that neither the first part of the Synoptic apocalypse (about the fall of Jerusalem) nor the second part (about the end catastrophe) represents more than the comments and expansions of scribes—their effort to say more fully what Jesus said more succinctly; what I think that this was I shall state shortly. And I do find this the best explanation of the discourse; I believe the presence of certain elements which I have mentioned makes it clear why the principles of this explanation are not immediately applicable to other discourses in which the same or similar elements do not appear. The end catastrophe is without much difficulty reduced to the common features of Jewish apocalyptic, and the Son of Man apparition is an obvious borrowing from Daniel 7:13-14. To conclude from this that Jesus said nothing about the end of the world would not only run contrary to the views of Albert Schweitzer but also to the opinion maintained by many of my contemporaries that Jesus is best described as an eschatological prophet. It more or less forces us to conclude that the non-eschatological Johannine Jesus is the most substantially truthful presentation of Jesus. If this were true, I would never have tried to write this book; for the Johannine Jesus is really unworldly.

We come, then, to the question of whether the eschatologism in which so much of the New Testament is steeped can and should be reduced to Jesus himself. I believe that it should; and I admit that it helps my thesis to say that it should be, so I cannot object to a critic who would say that here at least the conclusions have helped to formulate the argument. I shall leave the Revelation of John entirely out of this discussion, since I am satisfied that this book is derived from nothing Jesus ever said. But even without this collection of fragments from Jewish apocalyptic literature the amount of eschatologism in the New Testament is large enough and pervasive enough to suggest the need for some explanation apart from the fact that the writers were men of their times, and therefore shared generously in assorted popular eschatological beliefs. That is the way we deal with New Testament cosmology and New Testament demonology. About these things we say that we know better; I am not sure we can say that about eschatology. In denying any validity to New Testament eschatology we may have an axe to grind, or a face to save.

What did Paul mean when he wrote that the time (the useful time, the opportunity) is shortened; that marriage and celibacy, joy and grief, buying and selling (an odd assortment, surely) and the very "use" of this world are all impermanent? The reason given is that the *schema* of this world is passing (1 Corinthians 7:29-31). The context in which this remark is set is the context of the choice of marriage and celibacy, neither of which outlasts one's personal life; and no one ever thought they did. Is not the remark about the transitory character of the world and human life a bit heavy? Interpreters have generally taken this as an example of Paul's belief that the end of the world was near. But with or without this implication Paul's remark affirms that men and women achieve nothing enduring. To what extent does the remark go beyond Keats: "Look on my works, ye mighty and despair. The rest is silence." Keats, unlike Paul, did not write of an end which would be so total that there would not even be an observer to read and ponder the vanity of the inscription. It is not human life nor human achievements that is passing, but the *schema* of this world which is passing away (New American Bible: the world as we know it). It turns out to be a little difficult to find words for what Paul was trying to say.

The New Testament accepted the "day of the Lord" from the prophetic books of the Old Testament and converted it into the "day of the Son of Man" (Luke 17:24, 30) or the "day of God" (2 Peter 3:12) or the "day of Jesus Christ" (1 Corinthians 1:8; Philippians 1:6, 10; 2:16; 2 Corinthians 1:14; 1 Thessalonians 5:2, 4). This is certainly a mythological conception; but there are beliefs in realities which can be expressed only by myth. If one does not believe in the reality symbolized in myth, one should say so. The myth expresses a belief in a judgment of God which will declare finally the difference between good and evil—which may reduce the belief to its simplest terms. I cannot find such a belief incompatible with any kind of belief in God, and without some such belief I find myself compelled to say that there is no difference between good and evil, or that God does not know the difference, or does not care about it, or cannot do anything about it—all of which leave me without much of a God. That I have not the slightest idea how this will be accomplished does not entitle me to say that what I cannot think of, God cannot do. That would be mythology too. We may mention what is so often called the "last judgment" scene of Matthew 25:31-46. The common name is a misnomer. The passage places at the center of moral evaluation some actions and omissions which men and women are not accustomed to treat with the importance Jesus says they deserve. It is very significant, but it does not add to our consideration of what Jesus may have said about the end of the world.

The biblical event which interpreters call the *parousia* (Greek presence, arrival) draws its name from the ceremonial visits of kings (later of Roman emperors) to cities within their dominions. The name echoes the Old Testament coming of Yahweh to help, to save or to judge. The word (and the theme without the word) occurs in the Gospels (except John) to designate the coming of the Son of Man, described in terms borrowed from Daniel 7:13-14; he comes in the clouds of heaven and receives an everlasting dominion. Of themselves the words do not imply "the end of the world" (if one must be precise) but rather the end of a phase of world history; but the Synoptic apocalypse identifies the coming of the Son of Man with the end catastrophe of the world (Mark 13:24; Matthew 24:39; Luke 21:25-27). If these passages do not indicate the end of the world, what they describe will do until something more final appears. In the writings of Paul (both genuine and secondary) the Parousia appears as a fully developed theme which is assumed to be known to Paul's correspondents; and the genuine Pauline letters are earlier than 60 A.D., earlier than any of the Gospels. They thus attest the antiquity and the wide diffusion of the theme of the Parousia, and the independence of the theme from the historical events which terminated in the fall of Jerusalem in 70 A.D. The details of the Pauline theme (which I called developed) can be seen in 1 Thessalonians 3:13, 4:13 ff; 1 Corinthians 15:23; and in 2 Thessalonians 2:1-12 and Colossians 3:4, both regarded as secondary Pauline letters by many scholars. Similar allusions are found in the later deuteropauline epistles and in the Catholic epistles (which I do not cite explicitly). By the end of the first century the myth of the Parousia had developed even more fully into the myths of the final world judgment and the end catastrophe which is elaborated to the extreme in the Revelation of John. The myth seems to have been more enriched in Christian belief the more clearly Christians became convinced that the Parousia was not an imminent event, a conviction which has endured in Christianity until the present. I am not sure that modern Christians really believe in the Parousia or in the end catastrophe—or in eschatology at all.

I have called the Parousia a myth, and I have tried to explain that this does not deny to it meaning and value. I do not believe in the Second Coming as I believe in the first. This myth does not answer my questions about what Jesus said concerning the end of the world. The Parousia seems to be by all indications the effort of primitive Christians to express their belief in the ultimate vindication of truth and justice and the final victory of good over evil. I have that belief without the mythical expression. It is impossible, as I said earlier, to believe that Jesus said anything which denied the validity of that belief. We have other examples of the application by primitive Christians of Old Testament themes to Jesus which he did not himself apply; such would be the title of Messiah or the title of the Servant of the Lord or the theme of the atoning death. Of the theme of the Parousia now under discussion one may say that in a world where eschatology was a part of standard thought patterns the disciples found it necessary to make the Second Coming of Jesus the central eschatological event.

And this might very well be what happened, except that there remains some doubt about the degree of eschatological preoccupation in Palestinian and Alexandrian Judaism and no signs of it in the Hellenistic world in which Paul wrote his letters. Eschatology was present; but I am not sure that it was any more meaningful to the ordinary

Palestinian villager to whom Jesus proclaimed the reign of God or the ordinary lower-class resident of the Hellenistic cities to whom Paul proclaimed Jesus the Lord than it is to the ordinary citizens of European and American cities and small towns. Yet the gospel certainly has an eschatological thrust; without eschatology it seems unfinished. So what did Jesus say about the end of the world? If we read the Gospels as we must read them with modern learning, we are sure of nothing he said about the end of the world. What we are sure of is that he announced that God is finally establishing his reign. The consequences of that reign need not be the end of the world, but it will accomplish changes that will end a great many things. If the world refuses to accept the reign of God, may the consequences be terminal? I shall return to this question in the following chapter. But if we stick to what we can be fairly sure that Jesus said, we see that it left much room for the Christian imagination—as it leaves room for mine. It has been a constant theme of Christian imagination from the time when there first were Christians that when that imagination indulges in eschatological images it thinks with unfailing fertility of ways in which God would do well to hasten the eschatological process. I shall try to avoid this obvious trap, bearing in mind that serious reflection imposes the conviction that Jesus never said a word about the time or the signs of the end.

IX. NOT WITH A BANG BUT WITH A WHIMPER

Therefore a curse devours the earth,
And its inhabitants pay for their guilt;
Therefore they who dwell on earth are pale,
And few men are left;
The wine mourns, the vine languishes,
All the merry-hearted groan;
Stilled are the cheerful timbrels,
Ended the shouts of the jubilant,
Stilled is the cheerful harp.
Broken down is the city of chaos,
Shut against entry, every house.

—Isaiah 24:6-10.

WE have seen that it is possible that Jesus never said anything about "the end of the world," and that eschatology, especially of the apocalyptic variety, in the New Testament is entirely the work of redactors, the product of the imagination of early Christians who fueled their fantasies with material from Jewish apocalyptic literature. Certainly what we have learned about the age of the world and the age of the solar system, and even of the age of man, does not support that the collapse of the universe is upon us. Yet it seems to me that the announcement of the coming reign of God should make us uneasy about the worship of the bitch goddess Progress. Certainly God does not reign —or if he does, we know nothing about him. In fact we have gone a long way not only towards making it impossible for him to reign, but even impossible for him to survive as a meaningful reality. The announcement of his reign is

231

now 1900 years in the past; and if the ways of God are indeed mysterious, and if a thousand years are but a day in his sight, they are not so in our sight. It seems as irrational to try to explain why the reign of God has not burst upon us as it seems to be to say, as so many have said in centuries past, that it will not be long now. If one will forgive a cheap witticism, it is something like waiting for rain in west Texas.

Have we then failed entirely to grasp what Jesus meant by the reign of God? If we make it something so subtle that even after two thousand years of serious study and serious desire on the part of some pretty good Christians it still eludes us, how could Jesus have proclaimed it as good news to the poor, the weak and the lowly? They are still weak and lowly. If one believes that Jesus was a visionary and even worse, that he knowingly deluded others with promises that he knew would never be fulfilled, then tell me why he deserves any attention.

There may be an answer to this if we recall that the expected and awaited reign of God is not something to be achieved by God without the participation of men and women. Jesus has not only announced the reign of God, he has also shown the kind of people who make it possible for the reign of God to come to pass. God has only willing subjects in his reign, and men and women are not willing to listen to him. We human beings have not believed and do not believe that God can tell us anything about how to live and how to make the world a more suitable place for human beings to dwell together in peace and comfort. We do not perceive that those men and women who have submitted to the reign of God on the terms set down by Jesus have already entered into possession of the reign.

I have devoted several chapters to an attempt to set forth

how human beings have devised and sustain a vast system which in its essential features is opposed to all that Jesus said about how to live. It is not that God is slow to establish his reign, it is we who are slow to submit to it. Will he then impose it by force? That I do not believe that Jesus ever said. Neither did he say that God accepts defeat by human beings. Perhaps there are some things he leaves us to figure out. But an essential feature of the "teaching" of Jesus, slender as that teaching is, is that God is somehow involved in the human condition. Modern knowledge of the vastness of the universe has not, as many seem to think, furnished space in which an Epicurean God can hide or made it too big for any God to handle.

Therefore we have to ask what the "end of the world" might mean; and first of all, is it conceivable? Aristotle, once esteemed as "the master of them that know," thought that the world, the cosmos, by definition had neither a beginning nor an end. Thomas Aquinas, faithful student of Aristotle (in translation), accepted both the beginning and the end of the world on the authority of the Bible, although he insisted that reason unaided by revelation would be compelled to affirm the eternity of the world. Those who do not think the world will end can count Thomas Aquinas on their side as defending the rationality of their position. Thomas Aquinas was rather strong on insisting that God is not tied down by what human reason thinks God can or ought to do. I admire his wisdom, and I shall imitate his restraint. And therefore I shall say that the end of the world is inconceivable (as is its beginning), but I shall not say that therefore it is impossible; it simply lies outside rational discourse.

Can there not be cosmic catastrophes which lie outside recorded human experience? "One of our planets is missing." This is the stuff of science fiction, which may deserve no more and no less attention than cosmic mythology. What lies outside human experience exceeds rational discourse; and I think I have made clear my conviction that vast areas of reality lie outside human experience. Because the cosmic catastrophe lies there I doubt that it ever entered the discourses of Jesus, which stay rather close to the level of human experience.

Perhaps we shall be wiser and more practical if we think not of the universe or the solar system or even of the planet Earth (all of which tend to impose silence) but only of humanity and more precisely of that human phenomenon which I have been calling western civilization. An analogy may help us. All of us as individual persons are aware of our personal mortality. This is an insight which we do not share with the brutes. We do not think of it every hour or every minute (unless we are pathologically morbid), and in the normal health of youth or middle years we do not like to be reminded of it by things like the death of a contemporary (why are the deaths of contemporaries always untimely?). When one has counted 74 years one accepts the fact that one is a fugitive from the law of averages; but one does not brood about it. We die as individuals; but the show must go on without us. What we cannot imagine, cannot bear the thought of, is the empty theater—the landscape and the city streets with no one there. That is the stuff of nightmares; and that is the stuff which "the end of the world" forces into our minds.

But if Jesus did not say that God surrenders to human beings, neither did he say that it makes no difference whether human beings live as God wishes them or not. We are aware, of course, that the wrath of God is a biblical anthropomorphism; we do not seem to be equally aware that the justice, mercy, forgiveness, compassion and love of God are equally anthropopathisms. If we must have an anthropopathic God, let us at least do our best to make our anthropopathisms genuine efforts to describe the entire divine reality, not just those features which we find attractive. Jesus spoke much of the divine love and mercy, or so he was remembered; he was also remembered as speaking of the divine vindictive justice and the divine anger. We want a God who is all love—that is, he does not care what we do to each other. He is an amiable old patsy who allows his spoiled children to do whatever they please. When I read modern theology and—rarely, I admit—modern homiletics, I sometimes lay them down with the impression that Jesus never told a parable except the parable of the Prodigal Son. Anything else, like the parable of the merciless debtor (Matthew 21:21-24), cannot come from Sweet Jesus. So if Jesus did not predict the end of the world, imminent or remote, as a punishment for human sin, neither did he promise a hundredfold in this world and life in the world to come as a reward for it.

This is an attempt to set forth the feelings of reservation which I have in approaching the topics of eschatology, the end of the world and the final judgment. I admit that my feelings are confused because of the massive human failure to take God seriously and our habit of trivializing the life and death of Jesus. Whatever be one's Christology, one must believe (if one has any Christology) that the life and person of Jesus Christ meant more to the world than, for instance, my own and that this importance is reflected in whatever judgment God passes on me (if I believe that God judges me at all). If the biblical wrath of God is a valid symbol of something real, it is not to be trifled with or challenged. Did a famous royal house think they were God when they adopted as their motto, *Nemo me impune lacessit?*

With more than a little regret I think I am departing from some of the central ideas of one of the greater and more perceptive theologians of this century, the late Pierre Teilhard de Chardin. His understanding of God and humanity was dominated by his belief that evolution was an expression in nature and in life of the divine purpose that life should grow to fulfilment and that humanity moved by a certain cosmic inevitability towards its fulfilment in a condition which he called the Omega point of Christogenesis, when Christ, in the words of Paul, would become all in all. It is a spacious and inspiring vision. I found after a few years that it was too spacious for me, and that I could not share Teilhard's unbounded optimism. It seemed to me that his view took insufficient account of the history of humanity, that it failed to see the blood and dirt spilled all over the floor of history, that it did not see that Man whom Christ died to redeem (and whose redemption will be accomplished) is also the Bastard of the Cosmos, the only Satan there is. He seemed to be in no way disturbed by Man's evident unwillingness to be moved towards the Omega point. To me, if Man evolves towards becoming Christ by a process like that by which Man became a featherless biped, Man is saved because he is compelled to be, not because he freely accepts the saving love of God. I do not pretend to have done justice to Teilhard (who had known evil as I have never known it) by this too brief dismissal of a massive and well thought out synthesis. I do not think we differ at all in our basic belief that God is on our side. I think I am more aware than Teilhard that Man at least has to make room for God on his side. Some have said that a Jesuit-trained theologian always remains something of a Pelagian. Teilhard escaped it; I did not.

The theological perils of pointing out this or that as instances of God's wrath or of God's justice are many and great, and one wishes to steer clear of these perils. It is somewhat strange that we do not see the theological perils of saying easily and casually "Thank God" for what we believe are exhibitions of God's love and mercy, when we do not know that God's love and mercy had anything to do with it. It is probably because we find it easy to think of God as exhibiting love or mercy (towards us), less easy to think of him as exhibiting anger or justice (towards others), but we do not like to think of them even for others. With these things in mind, let us consider some realistic possibilities of the end of western civilization.

Arnold Toynbee counted, I think, 24 or 25 distinct cultures which deserve the name of civilization. Most of these ended by conquest; others died in the smothering embrace of a stronger culture to which they were assimilated. Of the Hellenistic-Roman civilization, the greatest of all up to its time, one may say, in the words of T. S. Eliot, that it ended not with a bang but with a whimper. There is no reason to think that western civilization has achieved an immortality denied to the much sturdier civilization of ancient Egypt, the records of which attest its continuous survival in its own distinct identity from 2850 B.C. to 31 B.C. The historian faces the death of his civilization with the same certainty with which he faces his own death. As others will take his place in the world, so the end of western civilization does not mean the end of the human race. The expected death of western civilization has a somewhat fanciful resemblance to the death of the dinosaur, which perished because it was too big for its world.

At this writing, our contemporary art form, television, recently drew the attention of its viewers to the recognition that the destruction of western civilization is now, it seems, within the range of human potentiality. This was shown in a television film called *The Day After*. The response of many politicians (I hesitate to give them the title of statesman) was that not one of them wanted this to happen. Most observers trained in the sciences said that the film failed to present the total horror of the disaster; they admitted also that it could not be presented in any art form. I believe in the sincerity of the politicians who assure me that they are as unwilling to risk this disaster as anyone. But what assurance do I have from the history of politics that there is any degree of folly or wickedness to which human beings in their mad quest for self-assertion will not stoop?

I do not, however, believe that the nuclear catastrophe for which we are heading will mean the end of human life or of all life, even though this may appear to be foolish and unfounded optimism. It is strange optimism to expect a catastrophe in which the few survivors will curse themselves and bless those who were instantly vaporized. The survivors will be wolves to each other; man is a survivor because he does what he has to do to survive. We really know very little about the details of the Black Plague which in 1347-1348 in some parts of Europe took off half the population or more, and a quarter of the population of the entire continent. By one of those ironies of human folly and wickedness England and France chose to hold the battle of Crecy in the year 1347. No one knows how many would die in a nuclear exchange; we know that it would be a greater blow than the human race has ever sustained, and that the civilized structures on which we depend without thinking about them would be shattered beyond repair.

Would it be total? I recall a member of the scientific fraternity who wrote about 30 years ago that the three species which have the best chance of surviving a nuclear exchange are the rat, the cockroach and the human. I suppose it would be misanthropic to note that all three are parasites; and I suppose it would be unscientific to ask whether the three could survive by living exclusively on each other. The behavior of men and women in lesser catastrophes is not encouraging for the prospects of a moral renewal through mass destruction. This feature was merely suggested in the film, not emphasized. It is one feature of the catastrophe which is within the reach of an art form; I wonder whether it was deliberate that the producers played it down.

In the early 1960s, in the first days of the atom bomb terror, a small discussion arose among Catholics concerning the right of self-defense against fugitives from the fallout who sought refuge in one's private shelter. It was maintained that such intruders might be repelled with deadly weapons and by taking their lives, if necessary. I wrote a letter to the editors of a magazine (*America,* I think) expressing my opinion that the good Jesuit who proposed this had made it abundantly clear that the thing to do in the event of an attack was to walk out to the lake shore (I lived in Chicago at the time) for a last look at the lake, the shore line and the sky. No attempt to survive in such a world would be worth making. Survivors are rarely moral heroes; but if they were people who lived by the ethics of survival, humanity would be dead in any case.

I admit that I have no more than a speculative theological basis for thinking that thermonuclear exchanges will not effect the end of human life, still less "the end of the world"; but if one must think the unthinkable, and it seems one must, one may project that it will bring about the end of western civilization if it happens. It may not be a sudden and dramatic total conclusion but, continuing to speculate, one may project that it will be a mortal blow which western civilization will not survive. I have some doubts about the validity of the projection of a complete cessation of life in all forms, higher and lower, on this planet as a consequence of thermonuclear exchanges. My reasons for doubting this projection, as I said, are no better than theological speculation. Since these considerations are not free from the anthropomorphism which seems to be inevitable when we talk about God, I am not sure that my thinking escapes romantic mythology.

My reason for my assurance of the survival of human life is quite simply that the extinction of human life would mean the defeat of God by forces hostile to God, and I mean no cosmic or superhuman powers; I mean human beings, men and women, people, us ourselves. I mean that if the human race can collectively kill itself it would assert its definitive power to deny and to thwart the will of God for the good of humankind. This may be the one point at which I feel safe in saying that God cannot let this happen. To risk a clear anthropomorphism, God has invested too much of himself in humanity to allow man to destroy himself. I say this is the one point where I feel safe with this assurance. Recorded history is loaded with events which by all rational calculation God should not have allowed to happen. If there is no power for good which is greater than the collective power of the human race for evil, there is no God anyway, so what the hell are we talking about? How God is to bring about this exercise of his power and will to save I have not the slightest idea. That he will intervene in history to avert the catastrophe is not to be expected; he has already intervened. About the Second Coming I have my doubts, as I said above, but not about the first coming.

Recently I heard a lecture delivered by the Rev. Robert Drinan, S. J., in which he proposed with skill and eloquence a way in which the intervention of God might be realized; I still say it would be a recognition of an intervention that has already happened. It would be unfair to say that Drinan treated the nuclear crisis as a purely political problem. But he spoke to a general audience where it can be presumed that most of those present saw the nuclear crisis as a political problem, and I believe his address was posed in terms he thought apt to win their attention—which he did. If the nuclear problem is a political problem, it can be solved politically. If it is a moral problem, it can be solved morally. If it is a human problem, it can be solved in no one of these ways. I think Drinan's solution must be labeled theological, although he was careful not to call it that. He hoped ("dream" was the word he used) that a sufficient number of people would heed the words of the pastoral letter of the American bishops on nuclear weapons and move effectively towards a negotiated agreement for the total abolition of these weapons. His earnest words carried conviction; he obviously believes that a public presentation can go no farther than this urging, which he called a "dream." I can do nothing but support his efforts. Why do I feel that this is not enough?

I suppose because the problem is being treated as a political problem and the bishops are being used as instruments of a political solution. By no means do I wish to imply that Drinan's vision is limited to the narrow horizon of politics; but with all due respect I ask leave to present a few other considerations. The nuclear problem I have called theological, and I have devoted this entire book to showing why I think so. I may be wrong, but I am not proved wrong by asserting that it is merely political. I think that the nuclear crisis is the acute and probably terminal phase of the moral fever which has gripped western civilized humanity. Jesus appeared to deliver humanity from this moral fever and he showed how humanity can emerge from the illness which I called terminal; and I think "terminal" expresses the meaning of the words of Jesus. If the bishops are truly the successors of the apostles, and if the Sovereign Pontiff wishes for once in the history of the papacy to place some meaning in what has been for centuries a title of mere vanity (I mean the title of Vicar of Christ), pope and bishops must proclaim the entire reality of Jesus Christ and his meaning to the contemporary world. In this crisis they must show that genuine reconciliation between the members of the human community is to be achieved not by power or by the imposition of the will of some upon others but by yielding. They must proclaim that western civilized men and women will escape the ultimate horror only by attending to the person and words of Jesus Christ. Like Paul, that is all they have to say; so for Christ's sake let us say it. And the first step we clergy might take towards this proclamation would be to become Christians ourselves. We can show that death to our cultural values is the beginning of genuine life; then perhaps we may persuade our fellow human beings that we too have a dream which can be realized.

What it comes to is this: because western civilization is such a blasphemy in the face of God, it will cease to exist, either because of the free choice of its members that it become something else or because its moral bankruptcy will destroy it. I have carefully avoided speaking of God's anger or God's judgment. The biblical myth tells us that God was willing to save Sodom for ten righteous people (the sin of Sodom was inhospitality, not "sodomy"). I think this is an incomplete (and therefore inaccurate) picture of God's wrath and God's judgment; but like all biblical myths, it can give us something to think about. And since the thoughts the myth evokes are rather somber, let us turn to the possibility that something like Drinan's dream comes to pass and that humankind escapes nuclear catastrophe and even removes nuclear energy from its armory. Would western civilization then be saved?

I am supposing that this development will occur on the purely political level—if it occurs at all. I will go further in my speculations: I will suppose that humankind discovers in the near future (or there will be no remote future) that it is as mad and wicked to settle international disputes by force of arms as it would be to renounce the police and the courts and leave the settlement of private disputes to brawls and murders. Desirable as such a state of affairs would be, I do not see that it would—any more than the abolition of private war and the presence of police and courts—abolish greed, exploitation, oppression and the quest for power, just the things which I have tried to set forth as the inner forces which are destroying western civilization. These things can be sought and achieved (and most frequently are) without recourse to private or social violence. If war were abolished, we, to borrow a phrase attributed to Jesus, have swept out the house to make room for seven devils worse than the one we expelled. I see nothing in a non-nuclear world which could compel me to remove or to alter any of the criticisms of our civilization stated in the preceding pages, nor to think that a non-nuclear or even a non-warring world would adhere substantially more closely to what Christians admit as the principles of life in society proposed by Jesus. I see international peace becoming a moral blanket to hide our nakedness while our moral derriere is shamelessly exposed. If western civilization does not blow itself into a noxious cloud, will it therefore escape other threats to its survival posed by its way of life?

These threats have grown bigger through the thousands of years of western civilization (including several thousand years which preceded its contemporary maturity). I am not unaware of the threats with which humanity has lived and successfully survived through these thousands of years, and which in modern times have been eliminated or substantially weakened. There is no question that certain epidemic diseases like the plague, smallpox, cholera and tuberculosis have been removed or rendered less dangerous—again, for some of us (although the quite contemporary and sophisticated plague of acquired immunity deficiency syndrome—AIDS—has sprung up with alarming suddenness in the very heart of western civilization). Many of us are better fed, better clothed, better housed and better enriched with the amenities of life than anyone ever was before. I will not dwell on the fact, because I have already been there, that life was good for 14,000 adult males in the population of 100,000 in ancient Athens. Nor shall I enlarge on the point that most of the amenities just mentioned seem to be mechanical toys, adult versions of children's playthings. It may be worth remarking that since I was born (in 1910, if you must know) the streets of American cities have become unsafe places for children to play and their elders to stroll. No, it would not be true that the world is worse than it was. Is it true that it is simply better? I do not know; with some doubts I raise the question.

I wish to avoid easy moralizing or cheap apocalyptic prophecy. I will therefore limit myself to projections for the future which have been made by so many others that they need no documentation. These projections do not imply any direct or explicit moral judgments on the civilized way of life; if the reader thinks that there are no implicit moral judgments, he or she cannot have read what I have written with very much attention. Let us first advert to the possibility (which some observers say is a certainty) that civilization will simply run out of space and materials which we need for a civilized life. I find statistics in this area about as meaningful as the national debt or interstellar distances, and I suspect that my readers do also. But I know no reason to question that statements made by many that the amount of fossil fuels is not inexhaustible, and that the recovery of some known resources is simply beyond the means of even wealthy nations—most of whose wealth is accumulated through fossil fuels. At the moment of this writing serious doubts are expressed about the use of nuclear fuels, and there appears to be a growing public sentiment against their use. How durable this protest will be when it becomes clear that there will be no power for such necessities as television, domestic appliances, heating and air conditioning, electronic music and, of course, food for our great god the Automobile, I do not know. I fear a sufficiently large number of people, when faced with a choice between instant privation and discomfort or remote danger of damage and great expense, will say the hell with the risks, living is for now.

We are, I learn from those who claim to be knowledgeable, plowing up or simply destroying or laying pavement over topsoil which it will take centuries of undisturbed repose to replace. One has only to think of the once fertile fields of Mesopotamia exploited by irrigation to realize that this is no empty threat. We do this to our soil not to meet our legitimate food needs nor to feed the starving here or elsewhere but to grow cash crops to be sold for civilized appetites. I have had occasion to pass some of our local supermarkets when the unsold food from the day past is thrown away. I am told that this obvious waste is now concealed; when I asked what happened to the unsold food, no one could tell me. The sheer hypocrisy of the shoppers at these markets who conduct marches about hunger is as revolting as the spoiled food, which the hungry would not be glad to get, but they would take it. After all, they would say, it beats starving. Pardon me if I fall into brief spells of moralizing. But I have retired to a state where some years ago one-tenth of the surface had been paved over; it may be more now. It is true that more than one-tenth of California will grow nothing more than chaparral and tumbleweed. It is also true that annually there is a run by thousands of motorcyclists over a stretch of the Mojave Desert. Experts assure us the desert surface is ruined beyond repair, although I admit that the unskilled observer like me cannot tell how the desert surface is ruined. But this blatant example of conspicuous consumption is a wonderful and pathetic example of grown men and women playing the fool. How empty their lives must be. One wonders whether there may not be something in the myth of an outraged nature avenging herself on those who raped her. Now I must write 100 times: "I must not moralize . . . I must not moralize . . . I must not moralize . . ."

Having written that, dare I risk another moral judgment by saying that our society is extravagantly, obscenely wasteful? Probably I may, since so many others have said it before me. I am concerned with the tons of rubbish and garbage which we throw away daily and with our prodigal use of water as if we did not know that by far the greatest part of the earth's water is loaded with salt, unfit to drink. But at the moment I am more interested in that form of waste which is seen in the diffusion of various noxious gases and floating particles of ash in the atmosphere. Humankind has come a long way since the first primitive human beings built a fire and spewed wood ash into presumably clean air. When I took part in an archaeological exploration many years ago, I was struck by the fact that some remote Palestinian had left a nearly ineradicable trace of his presence in a little ring of the ashes of a wood fire. Even the bones of himself and his family had in the course of probably 2500 to 3000 years been absorbed beyond trace in the organic cycle. Not the ashes of the wood fire which he built. I have been told, I do not know how correctly, that the bottles, cans and other types of manufactured waste left on the beaches and in parks will outlast by a few thousand years those who left them there—an immortal monument, like that of Ozymandias, to the slobs. But I digress, as it is easy to do on this topic. It used to be said, "as free as the air." We may be approaching a point of cultural advance where that will no longer be true, where unless we pay for clean filtered unpolluted air to be delivered for breathing in our homes, offices, stores and work places and to be carried in portable oxygen tanks by those who must venture out of doors (which few will do), the atmosphere itself may kill us. And where shall we dispose of the waste which we produce more abundantly than anything else? Shall we load the waste on satellites and put them into orbit (already suggested for the ashes of ourselves)?

Mr. Nevil Shute in his novel *On The Beach* has drawn an imaginary picture of the last days of humanity after the paroxysm of a nuclear war, "the thirty-minute war." In spite of the skill with which Mr. Shute has portrayed this, I have already expressed my opinion that nuclear war is not the ultimate catastrophe and that humankind will survive it, in what shape I prefer not to think. Mr. Shute has drawn vividly the breakdown of civilized society under the impact of a nuclear war, even though his fictional society was not directly involved in the war; it perishes because the rest of humanity has perished, and is the victim of a worldwide fallout. Were I writing the novel—which the world may join me in thanking God I have no intention of doing—I think fidelity to the probabilities would have made the end less peaceful; Mr. Shute's society dies fairly nobly. I have already made the point that perhaps that should not be expected. I was impressed by Mr. Shute's description of a society in its death throes in which no one is interested in garbage removal. In his novel human society dies like the aged, sick and abandoned who die alone smothered in their own wastes because they lack the strength and the will to sustain elementary hygiene. Who has not noticed that illness makes one wonderfully uninterested in cleanliness? Let us carry Mr. Shute's fancy a little bit farther and wonder whether our civilization, if it escapes its own nuclear bombs, may not die less dramatically smothered in its own wastes. Is it not possible that the wastes which we produce so prodigally may reach a point at which the collective consent of humanity is that it is just too much trouble to remove? After all, living is for now; it is more fun to lie on the beach and picnic on it than to clean up the mess we leave. Will we die suffocated of our own garbage because there is no one to take it out and dump it? This seems to me to be as likely an ultimate issue for western civilization as thermonuclear annihilation.

And thus we come by an obvious route to another possible problem of the future: who will take out the garbage? To put it in more general terms, who will do the dirty work? I said earlier that the only form of genuine wealth which endures through all cultural and political and social changes is an abundance of cheap unskilled labor. If western civilization has a genius, it is its unparalleled talent for exploiting the labor of human beings. If I had to choose one feature of that civilization as central, as the keystones of the arch, as that on which everything else depends, it would not be science or technology or engineering, it would be human engineering, the exploitation of people to assure the maximum output at the lowest unit cost. Modern human engineers are the successors of the slave drivers and the slave traders of less than 200 years ago. Cloning human beings is, as far as I know, only a gleam in the eye of some scientists. I am sure that they do not dream of cloning the living successors of Einstein or Picasso or Whitehead; what they are looking for and what will be funded are ways of cloning ditch-diggers, char-women, street cleaners, fruit and vegetable pickers and other necessary pillars of gracious civilized living.

I realize that by using the term "human engineers," which may be both pejorative and misused, I use a term which may have no clear antecedent; who are the human engineers? They are not a defined profession as such. I lump under that term all those in the modern world who participate in the movement of people from places where they live to places where there is work or the movement of work to places where people live. This sounds something like a description of people who operate the commuter transportation industry, and I do not mean them—although I do not know why I should exclude them.

Migrant agricultural workers do not commute from Mexico to California and Texas and the Middle West. They come and ultimately they stay, some willingly, others by processes which seem remarkably close to what was once called shanghaiing or kidnapping. I run no risk of being charged with inaccuracy if I say that all those who participate in this enterprise of human engineering are the successors of the slave raiders and the slave traders. I observe that I do not mean to exclude the commuter transportation industry; I say this because I was born and spent my boyhood years in the heart of the bituminous coal mining industry. Not all commuters are gentlemen in gray flannel suits riding the trains daily to and fro between the suburbs and offices in Wall Street or LaSalle Street. One of my earliest memories is the arrival of the miners' trains bringing them home from work between 5:30 and 6:00 P.M. They were so black with coal dust that they frightened us small children (the mines did not offer lavatory facilities). I was never up early enough to see the trains' departure (and the miners clean), which occurred by 5:00 A.M. Working time and pay did not begin until the head of the shaft was reached, and ended when it was left. This was an improvement over the older practice, when working time did not begin until the actual face of the coal was reached, and ended when it was left. I do not think the railroaders who manned the trains knew whose mantles they wore.

But in modern times we are not speaking of the slave trade. Until the 19th century workers were secured by raids and transportation was furnished by brokers who sold the workers to the owners near the place of work. The industrial revolution replaced the slave trade with the voluntary migration of workers, whose economic needs were so desperate that they paid for their own transportation. The cost was minimal, like the quality of the accommodations. The immigrant trains of the Union Pacific (called "Zulu trains" by the trainmen) gave that company a bad name, helped by Robert Louis Stevenson, for some years. The United States, to alter somewhat the famous lines of Emma Lazarus, asked Europe for its tired and poor and turned them into the huddled masses of its own industrial slums.

Now the descendants of these huddled masses who have made it to the end of the rainbow—which lies in the heart of the middle class—find that their fruited plains from sea to shining sea do not have more room for the tired and poor of other countries and continents who yearn to breathe free. Instead of repairing the Statue of Liberty we should remove it; it is a liar and always has been. The celebrated sign "No Irish Wanted" has been replaced by signs (metaphorical but real) which read "No _____ Wanted" (fill in as desired). Our land is not filled with brotherhood from sea to shining sea; to a long-time resident it looks as if it is filled with competitive hatred. Having done in the Native Americans, we have no one left to do in but each other, unless recent immigrants are available. While all this has been going on, we find that by promising everyone the opportunity to become middle class, we no longer have the tired, the poor, the huddled masses who will do the dirty work—or will not do it at the traditionally cheap rates.

I speak of my own country because it is the only one of which I have any experience. A reading of the daily press informs me that the countries of western Europe, which a hundred years ago shuffled off their huddled masses to North and South America, have in recent years recruited their cheap unskilled labor the way America did a hundred years ago. America promised its immigrants a kind of success which they could never have achieved at home; while the promise was illusory, it was real enough for some to keep the promise alive. Western European countries, which make no such illusory promises, have found their immigrant workers hard to digest. American immigrants were willing to wait for new waves of immigrants who made escape from poverty and low status possible by doing the dirty work which they hated. The story of American success is the story of someone standing on the fingers of the person on the rung just beneath him.

I do not think America ever solved this problem nor did it want to solve it. This country has always needed the lower classes; but no one wants to belong to them. The diffusion of prosperity, an unquestioned achievement of western civilization, and the consequent destruction of the lower class impose upon civilization the task of finding new recruits for the lower class or of forbidding emergence from the lower class to at least sufficient numbers of people to maintain a supply of cheap unskilled labor. This is the price we—more properly, someone else—must pay to sustain our cherished standards of living. I realize that this sounds like Swift's "Modest Proposal"; unlike Swift, I am not writing satire. In the United States we will continue to admit immigrant labor, legal or illegal. If the legal number of immigrants is not large enough, we will find it impossible to enforce the restrictions; we find it impossible now. But let us not deceive ourselves that we admit immigrant labor, legal or illegal, out of benevolence. This is the same benevolence our ancestors showed in the admission of Negro slaves, in their treatment of the Native Americans and in their opening of "the golden door" to fill the populations of mill towns and mining towns. We their descendants still like the products of cheap labor which we buy so cheaply. We closed the sweat shops in New York; we still support them in Hong Kong and Taiwan. But we are not responsible; these sweat shops are off our property.

It is probable that western civilization will not tolerate a resumption of the slave trade; I say probable, because the thinking and the ethics of western civilization give me nothing on which to found certainty. Against slave labor is the proved fact that it becomes uneconomic. Forced labor is another question. It would take very little of the ingenuity for which we admire our thinkers to serve up a version of forced labor under another name which our cultivated squeamishness would find morally tolerable. It would probably be presented as a program for the improvement of the welfare of the underprivileged, the "poor" of the Gospels, by transporting them to places where food and employment are available from their own countries or regions where neither can be found. I think this is a more likely way for western civilization to meet the labor shortage than the resumption of wars of conquest. The trouble with such a program is that the prospective immigrant laborers are not as docile as they were in the nineteenth century (the Molly Maguires were exceptional). They can smell the cooking in the kitchen of western civilization, and they will not easily be excluded from the dining room, as they must be if they are to remain forced labor. So we will hold our noses and detain them in labor camps, and let no one mention the words "concentration camps." They have heard of freedom and democracy; they may not know what they are, but it will take no education to see that they do not have them; and the affluence which they have learned to identify with the "democracies" they plainly do not have and are excluded from acquiring. No matter how the forced labor of the future (and I am not sure it is not already present) will be disguised, there will be civil unrest (the *stasis* of the Greeks) on an unprecedented scale. I suspect it will make the revolutions of France (1778) and Russia (1917) look like a game of touch football at a Sunday school picnic. That, more surely than thermonuclear bombs, will be the end of western civilization.

And if that were not enough, there seems very likely to arise an ever-growing shortage of raw materials and an ever-growing demand for them caused by an apparently unending upward spiral in the standard of living and a constant rise in the number of people who demand admission to the middle class. All these, which are not unreal or imaginary projections, add up to a ruthless competition for a shrinking pile of loot and a constantly growing number of people who demand a share. Perhaps civilized men and women will look more favorably on some of the more traditional means of population control, such as war, starvation and epidemic disease, or a judicious application of Swift's "Modest Proposal," or genocide; here in the United States we were doing it to Native Americans before any one ever heard of Hitler, and with such traditions it should not be too hard to resume it if we are pressed. I will be told, with the proper amount of disdainful scorn, that someone will do something about it before things are allowed to reach such a point. Something will be done, no doubt, by the same sort of wise men who are the lackeys of the establishment: financiers, politicians and scientists who have brought things to their present pass. I see no sign that the establishment is supporting the education of any other sort of wise men. The human race will go back to the caves and the forests, which will ultimately recover from the damage the human race has done them.

In the psychological depression of defeated Germany,

vanquished in the first World War, Oswald Spengler wrote a massive work called *Der Untergang des Abendlandes (The Decline of the West)*. The immediate future was worse than anything Spengler projected. But some aspects of his vision of the future were similar enough to my projections for me to borrow a paragraph from the closing pages of his work:

> With the end of the state, high history also lays itself down weary to sleep. Man becomes a plant again, adhering to the soil, dumb and enduring. The timeless village and the "eternal" peasant reappear, begetting children and burying seed in Mother Earth—a busy, not inadequate swarm, over which the tempest of soldier-emperors passingly blows. In the midst of the land lie the old world-cities, empty receptacles of an extinguished soul, in which a historyless mankind slowly nests itself. Men live from hand to mouth, with petty thrifts and petty fortunes, and endure. Masses are trampled on in the conflicts of the conquerors who contend for the power and spoil of this world, but the survivors fill up the gaps with a primitive fertility and suffer on. But while in the high places there is eternal alternance of victory and defeat, those in the depths pray with that mighty piety that has overcome all doubt forever. There, in the souls, world-peace, the peace of God, the bliss of grey-haired monks and hermits, is become actual—and there alone. It has awakened that depth in the endurance of suffering which the historical man in the thousand years of his development has never known. Only with the end of history does holy, still being reappear. It is a drama noble in its aimlessness, noble and aimless as the course of the stars, the rotation of the earth, and alternance of land and sea, of ice and virgin forest upon its face. We may marvel at it or we may lament it—but it is there.[1]

In a famous paragraph Macaulay once described the dome of San Pietro still standing as the seat of the Papacy at a time when some traveler from New Zealand would sit upon a broken pier of London Bridge to sketch the ruin of St. Paul's. Macaulay wrote this when it was Catholic teaching that the Roman See shared the indefectibility of the Catholic Church; this was still found in a modest *scholion* in the textbooks available when I studied this material (in 1937). I do not know whether this is still taught even in Rome. Insofar as the Roman Catholic Church has become identified with the fabric of western civilization it will perish with that civilization; and it worries me that its saints and scholars (I could be wrong here) have not been seriously concerned with how closely the Church has become identified with this civilization, which they should be able to recognize as the Anti-Christ. If the Church were to lose its papacy, its hierarchy, its clergy, its vast collection of buildings, its stores of learning amassed over the centuries, even the text of its sacred books and had to face the world with nothing but the living presence of the Risen Jesus and his living memory and its mission to proclaim the Good News to all nations and peoples, it would be no less a church than the church of Peter and Paul was. Perhaps it might be more of a church than it is now.

Some who have read this manuscript during its composition have warned me that such a lugubrious ending will alienate more readers than it will gain. Has anyone ever discovered a really cheerful way to announce that this ship is sinking? It does not seem to be a time to break out the champagne and celebrate, or call for music and dancing, or say "Living is for now," like the revelers in the Black Death. Could we ask ourselves whether we can at least die decently, or even whether we cannot make this last act a far, far better thing than we have ever done? How shall I convince my readers, if I still have any left, that I do not think of myself as bearing bad news? I suppose I have failed to convince that I really believe that the death of western civilization is not the death of the human race. If Jesus was right, only through that death can humanity die to itself and rise to a new life. That is a message of hope, not a wail of despair; that is the Good News which I hear proclaimed by Jesus Christ. By death to ourselves, which I have tried to describe, we shall be able to realize all the potentialities for goodness in human nature, come to fullness in the image of God in which we were made. The death of that tired world, weary in its wickedness, will be our salvation and our life.

I have said that we should not wait for God to intervene, either by a second coming or by anything else. God has already intervened in Jesus, and we need nothing more to fulfil ourselves. The disciples saw correctly that God has inaugurated his reign in Jesus. The word reign has misleading implications; it suggests that God imposes his will by a power which is uniquely divine. But Jesus proclaimed that the Reign of God is a Reign of Grace, that God moves men and women to their fulfilment by grace, by joining them to himself in a community of purpose freely and gladly accepted to achieve a richness of life in community never dreamed of in the shabby world of western civilization. Paul said: if God is on our side, what difference does it make who or what is on the other side? I have written this book in the conviction that God is on our side and has proved it beyond doubt. If that makes me a gloomy messenger of bad news, may I never hear any worse news.

NOTES

FOOTNOTES TO CHAPTER I

1. Robert Nisbet, *History of the Idea of Progress* (New York: Basic Books, 1980), pp. 317-318.
2. Pheme Perkins, *Commonweal* CXI (1984: 2), p. 51.

FOOTNOTE TO CHAPTER II

1. Karl Marx, *Capital,* Vol. I, Part VII, section 4 (Progress Publishers, Moscow, n. d., ET of 3d German edition, 1887), p. 605.

FOOTNOTE TO CHAPTER IV

1. Mark Twain, *The War Prayer,* Harper & Row, 1968.

FOOTNOTES TO CHAPTER V

1. Martin Dibelius, "Rom and die Christen in den ersten Jahrhunderte," in *Botschaft und die Geschichte,* vol. 2, pp. 177-228 (Tübingen: Mohr, 1956).
2. Walter Kaspar, *Jesus the Christ,* p. 107 (Burns & Oates/Paulist Press: New York, 1976).

FOOTNOTE TO CHAPTER VI

1. Hans Küng, *On Being A Christian* (tr. by Edward Quinn), Garden City: Doubleday, 1976, pp. 564-565.

FOOTNOTE TO CHAPTER VIII

1. John L. McKenzie, *A Theology of the Old Testament,* New York: Doubleday, 1974, p. 309.

FOOTNOTE TO CHAPTER IX

1. Oswald Spengler, *The Decline of the West,* vol. 2, *Perspectives of World History,* (ET: Knopf, New York, 1926), p. 435.